Life in the Legion

Life in the Legion

The Experiences of a British Volunteer
in the French Foreign Legion
in the Late 19th Century

Frederic Martyn

LEONAUR

Life in the Legion
The Experiences of a British Volunteer
in the French Foreign Legion
in the Late 19th Century
by Frederic Martyn

First published under the title
Life in the Legion

Leonaur is an imprint of Oakpast Ltd

ISBN: 978-0-85706-783-8 (hardcover)
ISBN: 978-0-85706-784-5 (softcover)

http://www.leonaur.com

Publisher's Notes

The views expressed in this book are not necessarily
those of the publisher.

Contents

Now I've come to my own again,
Fed, forgiven, and known again,
Claimed by bone of my bone again,
And sib to flesh of my flesh!
The fatted calf's been dressed for me,
But husks have greater zest for me,
I think that pigs are best for me,
I'd go to those styes afresh.

(With Apologies to Mr. Kipling.)

CHAPTER 1

Men Who Join the Legion

I have held a commission in the British Army and I have served in the ranks; I have been a traveller in strange places; I have lived a life full of vicissitude of sorts; and—I was for five strenuous and not unhappy years in the French Foreign Legion.

I am proud of having been a legionary, and it has hurt me to read the misleading account of life in the Legion given in a recent book written by a German deserter, who was admittedly but a few months in the corps and never got beyond the depot.

As the reviewers—among them a lady!!!—seem to have swallowed the German deserter's exaggerations without even a gulp, I would like to ask them if they would expect to get a dependable picture of life in a British regiment from a "King's Hard Bargain" who happened to be a native of a country with which we had a long outstanding account to settle some day. I imagine not.

The burden of the deserter's complaint is that the Legion is recruited from fugitives from justice and "hard cases" generally, and that life in it is so unbearably hard that every legionary is always on the lookout for an opportunity to desert.

Life in the Legion is certainly very far from being a bed of roses; but it must be remembered that the corps is always on service and that the lot of the pampered British soldier is not particularly downy in the same circumstances.

Fugitives from justice are indisputably to be found in the Legion, and, I may say, in pretty nearly every regiment of the British Army also. Perhaps the percentage is higher in the Legion, but it is certainly not high enough to warrant a song being made about it. Personally, if I wished to hide from the police of this or any other country, when they wanted badly to find me, I should be very careful indeed to keep away from the Legion—I rather fancy that it would be safer to try to get into the Metropolitan Police.

Broken men there are in the Legion in plenty; but they are not men to sneer at. Their very presence in the corps proves that no matter what their offences against social law and convention may have been they are still entitled to call themselves "men." Most of these social wrecks join the Legion from motives that more befit the character of a man than either patriotism, gain, or glory: they join to regain their self-respect.

There are men, too, who join from pure love of adventure; and of all recruits these are the least likely to be disappointed.

Lastly, among the foreigners, come those who enlist because they have been crossed in love. This is a fairly numerous class, and it furnishes most of the dissatisfied ones; for dissatisfaction is pretty sure to come when they realise, as they all do sooner or later, that they have done a very foolish thing in sentencing themselves to five years' hard labour because they cannot have the moon. I have never been disappointed in love myself—I sometimes think that it would have been better for me if I had been—so my opinion as to what is the best thing for a man to do in such circumstances is not worth much, but I think that if a blight of that sort fell upon me I should make haste to find another girl instead of inflicting unnecessary suffering on myself.

But the majority of men serving in the Foreign Legion are not foreigners at all from their own point-of-view. Something like half of the 8,000 men composing the Legion are Alsatians and Lorraines who insist that they are Frenchmen, although their birthplaces were annexed to Germany forty years ago. What do the Legionophobes say to this? To the indisputable fact that about half of the men who enlist into this "disreputable" corps are moved to do so by patriotic motives in their very purest form!

It was pure chance that led me to the Legion. I had been a fool and had altogether lost conceit in myself. I found that sleeping with my conscience, or trying to sleep with it, was very painful. I mourned over brilliant prospects thrown away, and I wanted to leave this weary world but hadn't the pluck to put myself out of mess. If I hadn't come across the Legion I should probably have taken to drink and ended up in the gutter. And my salvation came to me by chance.

I was in Paris, and one morning I was passing along the Rue St. Dominique in an aimless sort of way, feeling fairly "fed-up" with the company of my miserable thoughts, when a man emerging suddenly from a doorway, at the moment when I was maundering past, cannoned against me and nearly knocked me off my feet.

"Pardon, *monsieur*," he said, with a low bow and a genial smile.

I raised my hat and smiled in acknowledgment, and the stranger passed on.

He was a man of striking and distinguished appearance, and his manner, though courteous to an extent that would not be understood by an untraveled Englishman, was somewhat imperious and condescending. His dress, too, betokened class: I mentally decided that the fur coat he was wearing would have been cheap at a hundred guineas.

I stood staring after him for a minute or two, so much had his appearance impressed me, and then I turned to look at the building he had come out of.

The first thing that caught my eye was a big placard, headed with the "*Liberté, Egalité, Fraternité*," of the French Republic, stating that men between the ages of eighteen and forty would be accepted for service in "*La Légion étrangère*" and directed enquirers to walk inside.

I walked inside. The doorway led into the head recruiting office of the French Army, and as soon as I read that placard, which I should not have noticed if the man in the fur coat had not run against me, I determined to be a legionary if they would let me.

Going up to a booby-hutch that had the lettering "*Engagements Volontaires*," painted above it I, with some little difficulty, attracted the attention of a soldier who was writing in the office on the other side of the partition.

He appeared to me, in my ignorance of French badges of rank, to be a private soldier with two exaggerated gold good conduct badges on his arm, but he was in reality a sergeant-major—in the French Army a very important personage indeed.

"What is your pleasure, *monsieur?*" he asked politely when he at last came to the enquiry window.

"I wish to enlist in the *Légion étrangère*," I said briefly.

"Your name, age and nationality?"

When I had given him these particulars he directed me to go and stand outside a door lettered: "*Commandant de Recrutement*." After I had been there for perhaps a quarter of an hour the door was opened by the sergeant-major, who beckoned me to enter.

I found myself in a big bare office with a large table in the centre, at which was sitting a grizzled gentleman in uniform, with the *galons* of a colonel on his arm.

Without waiting for any instructions I marched across the room and stood "at attention" in front of him, after saluting in the orthodox military manner.

"*Bien!*" he ejaculated genially, as he looked at me approvingly. "So you have served already, is it not so? You know the ' position *militaire*,' and you have the bearing of a soldier."

"You are discerning, *mon colonel*," I replied. "I was for some years in a British hussar regiment."

He nodded amicably, as if he unreservedly accepted my statement and saluted me as a *confrère*.

"I am afraid that you will find life 'down there' very different from life in a British cavalry regiment; it is a great deal different from life in an ordinary French regiment for the matter of that," he remarked deprecatingly.

"It is understood, *mon colonel*."

"*Monsieur* has no doubt reflected over this step, and knows that the life will not appeal to anyone who does not love the soldiering trade for its own sake. There are many, too many, who join the Legion with no sort of qualification for a soldier's life, and these men do no good to themselves or to France by enlisting. I always try to impress upon every candidate that it is a step that should not be taken without much reflection." ' This is a peculiar sort of recruiting officer,' thought I; his manner was dissuasive instead of the opposite, and I wondered as I stood there if recruits for the Legion were so plentiful that recruiting officers could afford to choke them off in this way.

"I have reflected, *mon colonel*," I replied mendaciously.

Upon this he dropped the formal "*Monsieur*" and called me "*Mon enfant*," just as if I were already one of his own men.

"Ah!" he exclaimed, "you have done well, *mon enfant*. The Legion is a corps with glorious traditions and, to a soldier, to serve in it is a joy. Now, *mon enfant*, shall I be indiscreet in asking if you were an officer 'over there'?"

"I was, *mon colonel*."

"I was sure of it, and asked the question for a purpose. See you, the road to promotion in the Legion is broader and easier to travel to those who have worn epaulettes. Can you—pardon me, my friend, I have no personal doubts and am only fulfilling a duty imposed upon me by regulations can you give me any proofs?"

I hesitated. As a matter of fact, I couldn't give him any proofs that would fit in with the name he had before him.

"I fear I have been indiscreet," he went on. "*Monsieur* has doubtless borrowed a name, and in so doing has, perhaps, done rightly; but if the time comes, as I hope it will, when the colonel will talk about officer's rank, the *nom d'emprunt* must be discarded and the colonel taken into confidence. Till then one name is as good as another."

"You are good, *mon colonel*," I rejoined.

"Very well, then. You shall now go to see the doctor, and if he passes you as fit for service I will engage you."

He turned again to his papers, and the sergeant- major motioned me towards the door. I left the room with a high opinion of the urbanity of French officers, an opinion that became somewhat modified when I got to know them better, and found that the bulk was hardly equal to sample.

Then the sergeant-major ushered me into a waiting-room that was well-filled with a miscellaneous crowd of Frenchmen. These men were not conscripts, but recruits who had come up to join the army of their own accord so that they might get their military service over as early as possible, instead of letting the prospect dangle over their heads and interfere with the serious work of their lives.

Presently I was called into an inner room and told to strip. Then I was medically examined, not very strictly, I fancy, by a fat, genial surgeon-major wearing a pair of red uniform trousers and a white linen smock. While he was examining me he chucklingly chaffed me about my reasons for joining.

"These women! these women!" he said quizzically. "What fine recruiting-sergeants they are! How many engagements in the Legion would there be, I wonder, if it wasn't for women?"

"None at all, *monsieur le major*," I said with a smile, "nor in any other regiment either."

"You are too smart, *mon enfant*," said the doctor, shaking a fat fore-finger at me. "It is a terrible misfortune for a young man to be over-smart in any walk of life; but in the army it is calamitous, for a man who lets it be seen that he is smarter than his superior officer has a dog's life of it."

"*Pardon, monsieur le major*," I said deprecatingly. "I was merely referring to the fact that every soldier must have had a mother. My mother is the only woman who has had anything to do with my enlistment."

"Ah!" he ejaculated drily, and made no further remarks beyond such as were necessitated by the business in hand.

I knew the significance of that exclamation without any explanation: it meant that in his opinion a gentleman recruit who had not been driven to the Legion by an affair of the heart that had come undone, must have something disreputable in his past.

He passed me as being fit, and I was told to come again next day to be formally engaged, and sent off to join.

Next morning when I turned up I found the man in the fur coat sitting all by himself in a corner of the waiting-room, and when I reported myself to the non-commissioned-officer he told me that "that aristocrat there" was also a recruit for the Legion, and that I had better go and introduce myself, as we would be travelling companions.

I didn't do as he suggested, for I had the ordinary Englishman's dislike to making the first advances to a stranger.

After a tiresome wait of more than an hour a non-commissioned-officer came and bawled out my name and "Petrovski." The man in the fur coat got up and went with me into the room where the colonel sat. Here we signed an ordinary printed form, but what it contained I do not know, as Petrovski was called upon to sign first, and dashed off his signature without reading a word. In face of this I didn't care to stop to examine the document myself, so carelessly scrawled my signature likewise.

"You will proceed to Marseilles by tonight's train from the Gare de Lyon," said the colonel as soon as we had signed, "and you will be met on arrival by a non-commissioned-officer, who will give you further orders. If you should happen to miss this non-commissioned-officer you should ask your way to the military depot and report yourselves there. You must remember that you are now soldiers of France, and that failure to report yourselves will entail your being proceeded against as deserters. I wish you *bon voyage* and 'good luck.'"

Then he got up, leaned over the table, and held out his hand—I cannot imagine an English recruiting colonel shaking hands with a newly-enlisted private soldier.

The sergeant-major now took charge of us again and conducted us to the outer office. Here we were given railway warrants to Marseilles, documents establishing our identity as soldiers of *La Légion étrangère* travelling to join our depot in Algeria, and three *francs* each as subsistence money.

Each man got his own documents, so there was no necessity for us to travel in company unless we so desired; but we left the office together and there and then commenced a close comradeship that continued through our depot days to the times when we found ourselves standing shoulder to shoulder in many a tight place, and on many an exhausting march, only ceasing when we shook hands and vowed eternal friendship on the day when we were both honourably discharged from the Legion, wearing the coveted *médaille militaire*, which is the French equivalent for the English medal for "Distinguished Conduct in the Field."

As soon as we emerged from the recruiting offices into the street the man in the fur coat stopped and faced me.

"My friend, I am charmed to make your acquaintance," he said in faultless English, with the pleasing intonation that is given to our somewhat harsh language by some foreigners who learn it in the nursery. "Will it be agreeable to you that we spend our last afternoon and evening in Paris together? As you heard, within there, I call myself Ivan Petrovski; and I, on my side, heard you answer to the name of Fred Brown. We will not exchange cards, my dear Brown, because I haven't got one, and I don't suppose that you have one either."

He laughed heartily as he said this, and I laughed in response. Then he took my arm in the foreign fashion and we moved off in company.

When we made our way to the Paris-Lyon Mediterranean Railway that evening we were fresh from a *recherché* dinner at Cubat's, at that time probably the most expensive restaurant in Paris, and I felt as if I had known my companion for years instead of for less than twenty-four hours.

It is necessary to say that we had not only dined well but wisely, as otherwise the incident I am about to relate might engender doubts as to the sobriety of Petrovski, if not of myself.

The cabman who drove us to the station had a cough so bad that we could hear it above the sound of the traffic as we rolled along. When we arrived at our destination I looked at the man with some interest while Petrovski was paying him, and noticed that he was so poorly clad that he shivered with cold as he sat on the box.

I experienced a feeling of pity for the man, which might have prompted me to have given him an extra *franc* if I had been paying him, and was very flush of money at the time, but I couldn't imagine myself doing what Petrovski did, even if I had been a multi-millionaire.

He deliberately took off his fur coat and tossed it up to the cabman.

15

"Here, put this on, *cocher*, it will keep you warm," he said as non-chalantly as if he were merely giving the man a cigar.

The cabman stared at him open-mouthed, but made no move to touch the coat.

"Put it on, I say," said Petrovski, in an imperious tone that suggested his having been used to willing obedience.

The cabman laughed a short, bitter kind of laugh. "It's a poor joke, *monsieur*," he said.

Petrovski started forward as if he would pull the man off his box, and then suddenly turned round and walked into the station without another word.

'You could get a thousand *francs* on that coat at the *Mont de Piété*,' said I as I followed him. I had had my dealings with "my aunt," as the French name the national pawnshop, and knew what I was talking about.

He looked at me contemptuously and shrugged his shoulders. "You English think too much of money," he said.

"We don't put poor devils of cabmen in the way of being run in by the police for being in unlawful possession of expensive fur coats," I retorted tartly. "Who is going to believe that man when he tells the thieves' threadbare fairy tale about the coat being given to him by a gentleman unknown?"

"My God! I didn't think of that," he said as he rushed out of the station and shouted excitedly after the cabman.

But the cabby, who had resigned himself to the acceptance of the gift and was moving away, only whipped up his horse and departed as if he were trying the animal for the Grand Prix: he probably thought that the mad foreigner had changed his mind and wanted his coat back.

I have often speculated as to the further history of that cabman and that coat.

CHAPTER 2

Arrested

We made the journey to Marseilles in style, for Petrovski seemed to have money to burn, as the saying is, and had insisted upon paying first-class fares and the supplementary fare of about two pounds for sleeping berths. This appeared to me to be a wicked waste of fourteen or fifteen pounds, as the inconvenience of passing about twenty-four hours in the third-class of a slow train was nothing to men who had taken on our job, and I suggested that we ought to use our military railway warrants and save the fares for another day. But Petrovski waved my objections aside with a smile, and the remark that a sensible man never roughed it until he was obliged to do so. Consequently we travelled by quite a different train from the one we were supposed to take, which led indirectly to our roughing it in a way we little expected.

The first-class "*rapide*" landed us at Marseilles between nine and ten the next morning, some hours in advance of the time when our proper train would be due; and as the military authorities would naturally not expect recruits to travel by a train composed exclusively of first-class carriages we found no non-commissioned-officer awaiting us. This didn't distress us at all, as we had foreseen it, and arranged to pass the day in having a look round Marseilles, returning to the station in the evening in time to meet the train we ought to have travelled by, so that we could save the non-commissioned-officer detailed to meet us from disappointment. If we had carried out this arrangement all would doubtless have been well, but we didn't carry it out, and so got ourselves into what might have been serious trouble.

As soon as we got out of the train Petrosvki suggested that we should go and buy clean shirts and then make our way to a hotel to have a bath, change, and take *déjeuner*. I objected to the hotel part, saying that it seemed to me to be quite an unnecessary expense to take rooms for the day, as we should have to do, and that we could just as well change in a public Turkish bath and have *déjeuner* at an inexpensive *café*.

Petrovski snapped his fingers at this, a mannerism with him, and said that he didn't believe in making little economies when he had money in his pockets. I remarked drily that when two people travelled together the pace had to be that of the slower, and that if his pockets were bulging mine were not.

"Now look here, my friend," said he as he stopped suddenly and caught me by the arm. "We are to be close comrades, is it not so?"

I replied to the effect that such was my wish. "Very well then. Just come in here," he said, as he dragged me into a waiting-room.

"Now then," he continued, shoving me into a seat, "show me what money you have."

I produced about nine pounds, most of which came from the sale of my personal belongings the day before.

"Put it there," he said pointing to the table.

I laid the money down, and he took out his note case, which he emptied, afterwards turning out his pockets.

Then he made a heap of all the money and proceeded to count it.

"The total is two thousand three hundred and forty *francs*," he said, when he had finished. "Now we'll divide it equally and so put an end to the money argument."

This was carrying good nature to a length that I was not prepared for, and I absolutely refused to entertain the idea at all.

"Very well then, my friend," he said coolly. "You shall take your money back, and I will take an equal amount. As to the rest I will make a present of it to the first person we meet who appears to be in want of it."

From what I had already seen of him I quite believed that he would do this, and so I choked down my aversion to sponging and took the forty-odd pounds that was my "share" of the joint purse. It would be as well after all, I thought, that I should have control of some of his money, as I might possibly make it last longer than he would.

In thus dividing with me Petrovski was only, in a way, anticipating a time-honoured custom of the Legion, for we found out afterwards that when one man of a section had money it was expected as a matter of course that every member of that particular section should share in his good fortune in some way or other.

We now sallied out, and, after buying clean shirts and collars at the first outfitter's we came to, took rooms for the day at the Grand Hotel Noailles, where we had a sumptuous *déjeuner*.

Then, big cigar in mouth and feeling very well satisfied with ourselves, we strolled round the town and put the Legion altogether behind us for the time being.

We spent a very pleasant day; so pleasant that we did not like to bring it to a premature end, and agreed that we would not go to the railway station to meet the non-commissioned officer who would be awaiting the arrival of the slow train; but would have one last night of freedom and report ourselves at the military depot in the morning.

To be absent without leave on the first night of our military service was making a bad start, but we were broad-minded men and assumed that, even in the Legion, a recruit would be allowed to sin in ignorance—once.

We returned to the hotel to have dinner, and somewhat unfortunately, as it turned out, took our seats at a table next to one at which there was a party of young naval and military officers in uniform.

They were at the coffee stage when we entered, and had seemingly been dining none too wisely, for they were more larky and boisterous than is considered good form in a first-class hotel.

The waiter suggested in a whisper, and with a meaning glance at our neighbours, that we would be more comfortable at a table a little further removed from them, but we only smiled indulgently, and I said that the gentlemen were not likely to annoy us in the least.

I was mistaken in this, however, for we had not got through our soup before they commenced flirting pellets of bread at one another, and some of the missiles missed their marks and reached our table instead.

Petrovski seemed to be much more put out by this than the occasion warranted, and he called the waiter and told him to inform "those *gentlemen*" that their bread bullets were making bull's-eyes on us every time.

We saw the waiter go and speak to them, but what he said had no effect, for presently a pellet caught Petrovski full in the eye.

This made my friend lose control of himself. He stood up so quickly that he almost upset the table, and seizing the basket containing bread, which the waiter had left on our table, he launched the contents piece by piece at the offending officers, making very good shooting indeed.

It unfortunately happened that the greatest sufferer from this bombardment was an infantry officer who had taken no part in the breadthrowing, and he was naturally very much hurt in his feelings. He promptly came over to Petrovski and slapped his face without any preliminary request for an explanation, or any of the usual courtesies. It was only an open-handed slap, the sort of blow that an Englishman would consider sheer waste of time, but Petrovski went mad over it. He picked up his glass, which was full, and dashed the contents into the officer's face, sending the glass itself after it as a kind of afterthought.

This led to something like a free fight between we two and the six officers, and the manager sent for the police, who contented themselves with taking the names of the officers but marched us off to the lock-up, our names, presumably, not being considered good enough. We didn't stay in the hands of the police long, however, for when they came to search us, and found our Legion papers, they handed us over to the military authorities to be dealt with, and we were unceremoniously shoved into the *Salle de Police*, or prisoners' room, of the nearest barracks.

It was a discreditable sort of a row, and at the time I thought Petrovski was an ass to let his temper get the better of him to the extent he had done. I was certain that I could not have been caught in the same way, and I retained this opinion until a week or two ago, when I happened to be one of a party of four lunching at a restaurant in London, much frequented by visitors on account of its supposed historical associations. One of the party was a staid respectable solicitor, a man of much more equable temper than I am even in these days, and, in somewhat similar circumstances, he acted almost exactly as Petrovski had done. Since then I have not been so sure of myself, and intend to give festive hooligans who throw bread about a wide berth in future.

CHAPTER 3

Punishments in the Legion

The *Salle de Police* into which we were thrust to pass the night was a room about twenty-four feet by twelve, with a wooden guard-bed running along one of the longer sides.

On this place of repose there were stretched about a dozen soldiers with their clothes on, and about as many more were either sitting at the foot, walking about, or lying bunched up on the floor.

Our entrance seemed to cause a great deal of surprise, and the sergeant of the guard had no sooner closed the door on us than we found ourselves in the centre of a gesticulating group bent on finding out who we were and what had brought us there.

Petrovski was sulky and uncommunicative, but I told them shortly that we were recruits for the Legion who had been struck by some officers in a café row, and had taken the liberty of hitting back.

When they heard this there was much shrugging of shoulders, one or two grim laughs, and many murmurs of "Poor Devils," "*Conseil de Guerre*," "*Biribi*" and "*Zephyrs*."

"Eh, but they are droll, these *légionnaires*," said a wizened-looking rive-foot-nothing infantryman in a uniform that seemed to have been cast off by a much bigger man. "They want to join the Zephyrs right off. 'Blues' in the Zephyrs! *Oh, la! la!*" and he laughed until he was in serious danger of being choked by Petrovski.

Then I learned, in answer to enquiries, that a "Blue" was a recruit, and that the "Zephyrs" were punishment battalions stationed in the desert parts of Algeria, and consisting of the hardest cases in the whole French army.

I scouted the idea that we had done anything worthy of the Zephyrs, but I was grimly told that we should be lucky if we got off at that, seeing that the usual dose meted out to a soldier who struck an officer without hurting him was five years' *travaux forcés*, or penal servitude.

I began to be sorry that I had enlisted.

That was a very trying night: There was not room on the guard-bed for more than half of us, and the cell was so badly ventilated that as time wore on the atmosphere became absolutely poisonous. Petrovski had philosophically squatted down in one of the corners and seemed to sleep, but I never closed an eye. I passed the weary hours sitting on the floor in conversation with an intelligent little chap who seemed to be as wakeful and as uncomfortable as I was myself. From him I gathered that he and his comrades were undergoing a minor punishment called "*Salle de Police*," his particular dose of eight days having been awarded him by a sergeant because his rifle was alleged to be dirty.

In the British army nobody under the rank of company commander may punish a man, and the company commander's power is limited to awarding seven days' confinement to barracks; but in the French army non-commissioned-officers may inscribe a man's name in the "*Livre des Punitions*," and though the sentence is subject to confirmation and revision by the captain of the company and the commanding officer, who are supposed to inspect the *Punishment Book* every day, confirmation is never refused and revision is invariably in the direction of increasing the punishment, it being an article of faith with French officers that non-commissioned-officers must be supported unless they are so clearly in the wrong as to make backing them up a glaring injustice.

This system is no doubt responsible for a certain amount of petty tyranny, but, even with that drawback, it is, I think, much more conducive to military efficiency than the milk-and-water methods of dealing with private soldiers that obtain in our army. It makes the French non-commissioned-officer a much more important personage than his English prototype, for men who have the power of punishment must of necessity have more influence than those who have not, and the sense of responsibility it engenders makes the *sous-officer* a very dependable quantity when left to his own initiative in a tight corner.

While on the subject of punishments I may as well give full particulars regarding them, as such particulars will have to be given sooner or later.

The mildest punishment for an infraction of discipline is *corvée*, which is the French name for the pottering about barracks that in our army is called "Fatigue Duty." This punishment is dished out wholesale, the number of men undergoing it at one time being somewhat regulated by the demand for fatigue men: if there is a lot of work to be done there will be a lot of men sentenced to *corvée*. No fault can be found with this, for the work has to be done, and if there were not enough men sentenced to *corvée* to do it good soldiers would have to be impressed, which always causes great dissatisfaction.

The next punishment in the scale is "Room Arrest," which practically answers to our "Confinement to Barracks," with the exception that there is no punishment drill attached to it.

Then there is "*Salle de Police*," which also answers to our "Confinement to Barracks," with the difference that the men undergoing it have to sleep in their clothes, on the plank-bed in the guard-room.

It is within the power of the sergeant of the guard to make "Room Arrest" and "*Salle de Police*" very irksome indeed, for, as in our army, defaulters have to answer their names at the sound of the defaulters' call, which is blown at irregular times. I have known sergeants to keep the miserable defaulters on a perpetual run for hours together, by having the call blown every ten minutes or so, and, as failure to hear the call and answer one's name is invariably punished with imprisonment, a sergeant who sounds the call at less intervals than an hour is a well-cursed man.

"Ordinary Arrest" is a somewhat extraordinary punishment. Those undergoing it are kept in confinement all the time except when they are doing punishment drill, of which they get six hours daily. This is a very severe punishment indeed, which has no parallel in the British Army, and I am bound to say that it is often awarded for very trivial offences.

Then there is "Solitary Confinement," which is altogether different from anything that English people associate with the name: a legionary sentenced to "*cellule*" "is kept in the cell all the time of his sentence and never leaves it for any purpose whatever. He gets no exercise, has nothing to read, not even a Bible, and couldn't read it if he had, for his cell is in semi-darkness, his food is reduced to about a third of what a duty-man gets, and every other day he gets nothing but half-a-ration of dry bread, and the cells are veritable dog-kennels, being only about seven feet long and half as wide.

I have nothing to say in defence of this punishment. To stigmatise it as barbarous is to put the case far too mildly; it is absolutely inhuman. It is, however, reserved for serious offences, and a man can hardly get "*cellule*" without knowing what he is playing for. I have seen a recent story of a man who got sixty days of this punishment, but I fancy that this must be a mistake, as, in my time, no more than thirty days' "*cellule*" could be given, though, if the case was a very serious one, thirty days' "Ordinary Arrest" could be put on top of it.

The final punishment within the power of the colonel was deportation to the "Zephyrs" for six months, which meant six months of good conduct, as no man is allowed to return from the penal section unless he has been six months clear of a report.

If the colonel thinks that the case merits more severe punishment still, he sends the man before the "Council of War," or court-martial, which sits permanently at Oran; and there he may be sentenced to penal servitude or even death.

Any imprisonment by sentence of court-martial does not count for time, so that a man who might be unfortunate enough to get five years' penal servitude would have to serve his five years in the Legion in addition. The legionaries call this extra time "*Rabio*," or makeweight.

As to the punishment of the "*crapaudine*," or tying a man up until he resembles a frog and leaving him in the open, I really cannot see that the strong remarks that have been made about it are altogether just. No doubt the punishment is a brutal one; but I never saw it inflicted except once, and that was in the field. It seems to me that a general on service has only the choice between taking an offender's life or subjecting him to a punishment that must be brutal if it is to deter others from offending. I have seen British soldiers on service "pegged out" a punishment hardly less severe than the *crapaudine*.

After all, before howling about the severity of punishments in the Legion, it is necessary to remember that it is not a feather-bed crowd, and that punishments, to be effective, must be adapted to the thickness of the skin that they have to get through. Such punishments as are inflicted in the British Army for serious offences would not, in most cases, be severe enough to act as a deterrent upon men of the Legion.

CHAPTER 4

A Mixed Lot

The next morning we were marched, in charge of an armed escort, along the busy water front to an old fort with a curious old lighthouse tower and a drawbridge. This was Fort St. Jean, which at that time was supposed, in connection with another decrepit-looking construction called Fort St. Nicholas, to defend the entrance to the harbour of Marseilles. I was told that the fort derived its name from the fact that it originally belonged to the Knights of St. John of Jerusalem, and there cannot be any doubt that parts of it are very ancient, but the fortifications seemed to me to be of a very distinct seventeenth century type, and I question very much if the Knights of Malta had anything to do with them. At the time I am writing of, the fort not only served as a halting place for Chasseurs d'Afrique, Legionaries, and *sous-officers* of *Spahis* and *Turcos* on their way to Algeria; but it was also used as a military prison for troops of the home army, and as a convalescent depot for men invalided from Algeria for change of air.

The corporal of the escort was very surly, and we could get no opinion from him as to what was in store for us, but his manner was not reassuring, and it was evident that if he had told us his thoughts they would have indicated that we were in for a warm time.

I myself didn't think it possible that we could get off lightly, because even in our army the officer is always in the right, and I thought that this was certain to be more so in the French service. The Russian didn't seem to be worrying himself much, and merely remarked, when I asked him what he thought they would do with us, that he hoped they would give us some breakfast before leading us out to execution.

Our escort handed us over to the sergeant of the guard, who didn't seem to know what to do with us, and took us to the *adjudant* on duty.

I may here remark that an *adjudant* in the French army is not at all the counterpart of an adjutant in the British service, though the translation is given in all the dictionaries. In the British army an *adjutant* is a big pot indeed, who practically commands a regiment, in matters of detail, by means of the Shibboleth, "By Order"; but in the French army an *adjudant* is not a commissioned officer at all, and does not even rank as high as a warrant officer does with us, though he is sometimes addressed as "*mon lieutenant.*"

As I write the word "*adjudant*" there comes to my mind a gallant fellow who held that grade in the Legion. If there was any fighting going on he was always on the premises, and it was a pretty regular thing to find complimentary mention of him in orders on the day following a skirmish or a battle. He was borne on the rolls of the Legion as a Belgian, but, as will be seen, he was a Frenchman who had adopted the Belgian nationality so that he could enlist into the Legion without producing his papers, as Frenchmen have to do.

When I was discharged I left him in the Legion, and thought that he had passed out of my life altogether, but he was brought into it again in rather a curious fashion. Some years after I had left the Legion I happened to be in Chalons, and got into conversation with an infantry sergeant, who, when he heard that I had served under the tricolour, volunteered the information that an *adjudant* of my old corps was to be tried by the local "Council of War" on the following day. I asked the man's name, but it conveyed nothing to me, and my interest evaporated.

Next morning, however, when taking a walk, I came full tilt against a military prisoner in the uniform of an *adjudant* of the Legion and wearing the *medaille militaire*, with other decorations. I didn't need to look at the prisoner twice; it was the Belgian.

I turned round and followed to the court, to which I had no difficulty in gaining admittance, and there I heard a wonderful story that sounded more like fiction than sober fact.

The evidence was to the effect that the accused had been a sergeant-major in an infantry regiment stationed at Verdun, I think it was, and that, having misused public money entrusted to his charge, he deserted and enlisted in the Legion under a false name and nationality. He was tried in his absence and sentenced to twenty years' penal servitude. Now, having been honourably retired from the Legion with a pension after fifteen years' service, he had straightway returned to

Verdun, repaid the money he had embezzled, and voluntarily given himself up to the military authorities to undergo his punishment. It was ordered that he should be re-tried, and it was this new trial that was now in progress.

The court was composed of a colonel, a commandant, a captain, a lieutenant, a sub-lieutenant, and an *adjudant*—there is always a non-commissioned-officer on a French court-martial when the accused is a non-commissioned-officer or private—and they sat in a row on a magisterial bench, not round a table as in England. At either end of the row of officers stood a sentry in full dress with fixed bayonet.

When the evidence and the speeches of the government commissary, also an officer, and the counsel for the prisoner had come to an end, the court retired to deliberate.

They were absent but a few minutes when a sergeant in uniform, who acted as usher, suddenly called out: "The Council."

Instantly everybody in court stood up, and as the members of the court filed in again the sentries presented arms.

The members of the court took their places as before, the juniors farthest away from the president, but they remained standing, and with their heads covered.

"In the name of the French People," said the colonel, and the members of the court carried their hands to their *kepis* in salute.

"The court find the prisoner ' Not Guilty ' without a dissentient voice, and order his immediate release from custody," the colonel continued.

Then they filed out again, and the proceedings were over.

I am happy to say that I was one of the first to shake my old comrade by the hand, and that we had a very merry dinner together that night. That is the sort of "wrong 'un" one finds in the Legion.

In strict justice he ought not to have been acquitted, of course, for he had undoubtedly been guilty of embezzlement, and his acquittal by a British court-martial would have been practically impossible; but the French are very susceptible to sentiment, and it was no doubt repugnant to the feelings of the members of the court to put a stain on the character of a brave soldier that no pardon or remission of punishment could efface. In England he would certainly have been convicted, though the punishment would in all probability have been remitted by the confirming authority, and the conviction would have been remembered long after the splendid expiation had been forgotten.

That is rather a long digression from the main track of my story, but I am not one of those who find the pen more comfortable in my hand than the sword, and I think I can tell my story best in this discursive and informal way.

Well, to get back to my story, the *adjudant* of the week looked at the documents that had been handed over with us, and then looked curiously at us.

"Have you spent all your money?" he asked mockingly.

"No, *monsieur*," I replied.

"Don't '*monsieur*' me," he retorted sharply. "I'm no lousy *pekin* (civilian) that you should talk to me in that way. I've a handle to my name that I've earned. I'm '*monsieur l'adjudant*' and you'll do well to remember it."

"It shall be so, *monsieur l'adjudant*," I replied meekly.

"What brought you to the Legion if you have money left after paying your own fares from Paris and cutting a dash at the best hotel in the place?"

"We enlisted for the fun of the thing, *monsieur l'adjudant*," I replied.

"*Nom d'un pipe!* you're a pair of humorous devils right enough, if you can see any fun in the Legion," he said grimly. "Take them over to the *Salle des Rapports*, sergeant, and keep them there until *monsieur le commandant* sees them."

We saw *monsieur le commandant* in due course, and I thought I saw him again a year or two ago on the stage in *The Second in Command*, for he was the very spit of the fine fellow who is the hero of that play as personated by Cyril Maude, with the exceptions that his hair was trimmed brush fashion and he wore red breeches.

Petrovski in his best grand *seigneur* manner was proceeding to argue out the matter of the assault on the officers, when the major held up his hand.

"I know nothing of that," he said, "and I don't want to know anything about it. The police simply charge you with creating a disturbance in the hotel, and I, personally, want to know why you didn't report yourselves to the non-commissioned-officer at the railway-station."

I thought that I could manage this development better than Petrovski, and so I chipped in before he could open his mouth.

"But certainly we are culpable, *mon commandant*, and have nothing to say beyond making an appeal to your benevolence," I said, deprecatingly. "We had hoped to make a career in the Legion, and if you take a serious view of the matter it will be the spoiling of two good soldiers."

"I believe you, *mes enfants*," he said, graciously, "and I am not going to take any notice of it at all; but remember when you are amusing yourselves in future to keep away from places frequented by officers. *Rompez* (dismiss)."

"*Nom de Dieu!* But you are two lucky numbers," said the sergeant when we got outside. "You ought to drink the commandant's health."

"Come and crack a bottle with us," said Petrovski impulsively.

The sergeant shook his head. "No, my good comrades, that is not allowed," he said; "but I could perhaps find another sergeant to share a litre with me if I had the money."

Petrovski, who did everything *en prince*, promptly responded to this hint by pressing a twenty-*franc* piece into the sergeant's palm, much to the non-com.'s astonishment. He probably expected a franc, which would have been sufficient to have bought half-a-dozen bottles of canteen wine, quite as good wine, by the way, as one would pay two shillings a bottle for in an English restaurant.

This was our introduction to the fact that non-commissioned-officers in the French army are open to be tipped. It has to be done delicately though, and the tipping is usually done by asking their acceptance of presents in kind, or, better still, by leaving the presents where they can find them. A packet of cigarettes, or of tobacco, a bundle of cigars, or a bottle of sealed wine, will never offend a sergeant or a corporal if given by a good soldier who is not likely to expect anything more than goodwill in return, but the goodwill of a non-commissioned-officer is very useful sometimes, and his ill-will is a misfortune always.

Let it not be inferred from this that it is necessary to bribe non-commissioned-officers in order to get them to treat one with decency, or that I personally made my way in the Legion by means of "creeping," because that is very far from the truth. It was generally the non-commissioned-officers who were most popular by reason of their fairness that received little attentions like this when a legionary got money from home, and though I did make many trifling gifts to non-commissioned-officers I don't think that I ever gave for any reason other than that which prompted me to buy wine or tobacco for my equals—in my time in the Legion nobody need go without a drink or a smoke as long as there was any one in his section who had tobacco or money.

The sergeant handed us over to a corporal, who conducted us to a barrack room, in which we found about a dozen men in plain clothes like ourselves. These were recruits for the Legion who had enlisted in provincial towns, no fewer than eight of them having come from Belfort, which, by reason of its proximity to the German frontier, seems to send more recruits to the Legion than any other place.

They were a very mixed lot indeed, and some of them seemed to be already regretting their bargains, if one could assume as much from their glum countenances. Afterwards, on board the boat, I got into conversation with two of these gloomy ones, and they told me an extraordinary story of their having been arrested on a trumped- up charge by the French police, and been given the choice between going to prison and joining the Legion.

I couldn't reconcile this tale with the recruiting officer trying to dissuade me from joining, and I don't believe it now, but I am bound to say that I heard much the same thing from others later on.

These two men were Germans, and, like many of their countrymen in the Legion, they turned out to be very unsatisfactory soldiers. They eventually deserted, and, after terrible hardships and many narrow escapes from the wild tribes of Morocco, got to Tangiers. Here they managed, with the assistance of a member of the crew, to stow away on an English steamer that was going to Malta and the Levant; but, unfortunately for them, the ship had to call at Algiers, and the captain, having in the meantime discovered their presence on board and not sympathising with them, handed them over to the French authorities, who promptly handcuffed them to a gendarme apiece and sent them back to the Legion. What terrible hard luck that was! And what a little thing brought it about!

If they had not met that benevolent member of the English steamer's crew they would have gone to the German consul, for they had already decided on that step, and he would have sent them home— consuls only refuse to help legionaries while they are on French territory—or if the benevolent individual's ship had been on its homeward instead of its outward voyage they would have got to Liverpool in place of getting to Algiers. I happened to be on guard when they were brought back, and I shall never forget the pity I felt for them when they told me their heartbreaking story of the sufferings they had undergone during their two months' absence. If they told that English captain anything like the tale they told me he must have been a flinty-hearted character to send the poor devils back. They were tried by court-martial, got two years' penal servitude each, and I never saw or heard anything more of them.

There was another member of that party of recruits whose after career was interesting in a different way. He didn't at all seem to fit his surroundings as I saw him for the first time that morning in the barrack-room at Fort St. Jean waiting for the morning "soup." He was dressed in an irreproachable frock coat, with an equally faultless pair of grey trousers, and his boots and tall hat were as shiny and correct as they make them. But what puzzled me most and raised my envy, at first sight of him, was the fact that he was wearing a shirt that was clean and glossy from the hands of the laundress. I couldn't understand that at all until we formed up that afternoon to be marched down to the boat, and then he appeared on parade carrying a portmanteau, and the mystery was solved. Fancy a man enlisting in the Foreign Legion and bringing a portmanteau with him! He was supercilious, standoff-ish, and disdainful in his manner, and I always felt like a pitiful worm beside him; but for all this, and though he was the most unpopular man I knew in the Legion, he was a rattling good soldier, and knew the trade from A to Z.

What country owned, or disowned, him, I don't know; but it was rumoured that he had been an officer of the Austro-Hungarian General Staff, and it was chaffingly suggested that he was, perhaps, the missing Austrian archduke. He was certainly "stuck-up" enough to be an emperor, But, whatever he was, there could be no doubt of his being a man of extraordinary grit and resource, for he extricated a convoy in Tonquin from a most difficult position and was, most deservedly, promoted to a commission.

There was yet another of that crowd who deserves a few words. He was an outsider as far as apparel went, for he was literally in rags; but he was an easy first favourite, both then and afterwards, as regards popularity, for he was one of those rare men that one seems to know intimately after having been in his company for five minutes. I don't think that I ever saw that man without a smile on his face—in fact, his nickname in the Legion was "The Smiling Swiss," and it used to be said that he couldn't look serious if he tried. He was the most good-humoured, simple, lovable lump of a man I ever met in my life—and he was the only man I ever heard of who made a fortune in the Legion. He became "*ordonnance*," or soldier-servant, to his captain, whom he accompanied on a visit to Algiers, and there he fell in with a wealthy French widow, who married him. That widow was a lucky woman.

We had not been in the barrack-room more than five minutes when a bugle sounded outside, and the corporal took two of the men away with him, presently returning with a wooden carrying tray containing mess tins and small loaves of bread.

I looked on anxiously while he was serving out the tins and the loaves, for I was very hungry and was doubtful as to whether I should find myself "in mess"; but my fears were groundless, and I soon found myself trying to eat thick potato stew by the sole aid of my pocket-knife.

It was not at all bad, that stew, or "soup" as they call it, and I made a very satisfactory meal, while hoping that I should get nothing worse "over there."

After "soup" we invited our new comrades to come to the canteen to drink to our better acquaintance, and all of them but one accepted with alacrity. The exception was the swell in the frock coat, who politely, but freezingly, said that he did not desire to drink when Petrovski wound up his heavenly smile and asked him. Petrovski bowed and, as far as I know, never spoke to the man again.

We passed a joyous time in the canteen, filling up *Spahis*, *Turcos*, *Chasseurs*, and legionaries indiscriminately at a ridiculously small expense, for wine in a French canteen is cheaper than beer is in an English one, and stayed there until the corporal came, at about three o'clock, to rout us out to go down to the boat.

There were a lot of recruits at Fort St. Jean for the ordinary African corps of the French army, and more than a few bad characters bound for the Zephyrs, but it was only we of the Legion that went by the mail packet that day.

As the boat passed the Château d'If the universality of *Monte Christo* was brought home to me by the fact that every man of our cosmopolitan crowd looked at it with interest, and seemed to be well acquainted with the story of the escape. Then, just as we were clearing the harbour, there was another sight, one that brought a lump to my throat and made me intensely dissatisfied with myself: it was the British Mediterranean Fleet, with the Union Jack at every bow, and the cross of St. George floating proudly over every stern. I felt that I had wilfully thrown away my birthright: I had no concern with that flag for the next five years at least. I was a despicable renegade.

CHAPTER 5

Oran

We left Marseilles between five and six on a Thursday evening and arrived at Oran just before noon on the following Saturday.

Oran is strongly fortified, but from the sea it looks so glaringly inoffensive and helpless that anyone who judged its defences by what could be seen would have no hesitation in betting that it could be taken by a torpedo boat.

As soon as the packet touched the wharf a sergeant of the Legion came on board and marched up to the forepart of the boat, where we were congregated looking over the side.

"*Légionnaires à moi*"—legionaries come to me—he shouted in a strident parade voice as he stood in the middle of the deck and raised his right arm above his head.

This struck me as being a somewhat silly proceeding, seeing that at least half of our party had no knowledge of French, but it answered all right, and after checking us off on a kind of way-bill he marched us off the ship, through the wide well scavengered streets of the town to Fort St. Theresa, which lies on a hill some distance behind.

We must have looked curiously out of place, we fifteen men in assorted European clothes, as we marched through the throng of negroes, dark-skinned Arab men, and olive-complexioned Algerian women; but we didn't seem to interest the populace a little bit. This surprised me at the time, but I ceased to wonder when the sergeant told me that about a hundred recruits passed through Oran in this way every week in the year. Just think of that: four or five thousand recruits per annum to fill the gaps in a force which never numbers more than twelve thousand and seldom exceeds eight thousand! What an object lesson as to the risks of service in the Legion!

"How much farther, *mon sergeant?*" asked Petrovski, who seemed to be a bit out of training and blown by the long uphill tramp.

"Just a bagatelle: about a kilometre," replied the sergeant, looking at him curiously. "They'll soon teach you 'down there' to do thirty kilometres carrying a donkey-load on your back with less trouble than this little bit seems to be giving you."

"*Ma foi*, I'm afraid they won't do anything of the sort if the kilometres 'down there' stand up on end like they do here," rejoined Petrovski.

"You'll see, my friend, you'll see," said the sergeant grimly.

I thought of this later when I used to see poor Petrovski doubling round and round the exercise-ground with the squad, puffing and blowing most distressfully, and shedding his fat by the pint.

When we got to the fort we were inspected by an officer, and then shown into a dark filthy hole that might have been a *salle de police* at some time or other. The wooden guard-bed, on which there was a pile of dirty looking blankets, was the only fitting the room contained, and as soon as I saw the accommodation I not unnaturally jumped to the conclusion that this was the sort of thing we were to expect for the next five years, and was not at all pleased with the idea.

Being left to our own devices, after being cautioned against leaving the fort, Petrovski and I speedily found our way to the canteen and invited two thirsty-looking legionaries whom we found standing outside to show us the ropes.

They accepted the job with alacrity, and the trifle we spent filling them up with good red wine of Algeria was an excellent investment; for they were a couple of merry fellows and, besides giving us much useful information, entertained us hugely with yarns of Legion life in camp and barracks. Most of their stories had a woman in them somewhere, but there was one that may well be reproduced here, especially as it happens to be true, in its main facts at any rate, though it may sound unconvincing.

One of them was wearing a medal, and I asked him what it was for.

"Oh!" laughed the other one, "he got that for pinching the general's clothes."

"Yes, that's right," said the man with the medal, grinning: "but it is you, my worthy man, who ought to be wearing it."

"Have another litre and tell us about it," I suggested.

"Eh, but you are good recruits," he remarked appreciatively as he held out his hand for the money. "We don't get many *bons camarades* like you come through here."

"So you want to know how I got this bit of *ferblanterie* (tinware), eh?" he asked, as he settled himself in front of the fresh bottles and lighted his pipe, which he had filled from a packet of tobacco he had bought with our money without asking. I nodded assent.

"Well, it was owing to a general, who called himself Louis, but ought to have been named '*Cochon*' (pig). He didn't like the Legion, and when he was in command of our brigade on the manoeuvres of '82, he made us feel it. He annoyed us, and some of the boys made up their minds to annoy him. One fine morning, at the first note of reveille, he wriggled out of his sleeping-sack and looked for his breeches. They had disappeared, and so had every other bit of his clothing, and his camp equipment: he had nothing but what he stood up in, and that wasn't nearly enough to command a brigade in. Somebody had got into his tent, although there were two sentries of the Legion posted there all night, and made off with the whole of his kit. There was a terrible row, and the camp and every soldier in it was searched, but not a single article was found—and they never have been found to this day.

"The general was annoyed right enough, and the Legion was avenged when he appeared on parade looking a figure of fun in clothes borrowed from men bigger and smaller than himself. Oh, it was a gay sight, and even the officers hurt themselves trying to look solemn when they wanted to laugh. I had the bad luck to be on guard that night, and it was the guard that had to pay for all the fun. My friend Jules here was not of the guard, and though he had more of the fun than I had he had to pay nothing. I was sent away, with the others of the guard, to the extreme south, on the borders of the desert, and found myself in a miserable little blockhouse on an oasis a mile or two from Ras-el-Chel, at that time the worst station in the whole Legion.

"There were ten of us, with a sergeant and a bugler, in that blockhouse and we had nothing to do.

"It is not good to have nothing to do, and, at first, I thought that I would rather have been sent to the Zephyrs than to that blockhouse; but I was mistaken, for I hadn't been there very long before the Oulad-Seghir Arabs made us as busy as we wanted to be.

"It was at Noël that they came down on us, thinking, no doubt, that as we generally got a few litres extra under our cartridge boxes at Christmas-time, they would have a better chance with us then.

"We of the blockhouse had a good supply of wine on that Christmas Day. I got four or five litres myself (7-9 pints) and when I went to sleep I wanted to stop asleep for a long time. But I didn't get a chance, because in the middle of the night the sergeant, who was a poor man at the drink, came and shook us until we roused up. We had no sooner opened our eyes than we heard the bugler on the roof cracking his lungs with the 'rouse,' the 'alarm' and the 'regimental call.'

"We bounded up to the roof with our rifles in our hands, but no trousers on our legs, and lined up at the 'ready.'

"'Good,' said the sergeant, 'I was afraid that you were all too drunk. I came up here to smoke a pipe and found that the sentry had gone to bed with the rest of you. It would have been a bad job for us if I hadn't wanted that pipe. Look there!' and he pointed to the borders of the oasis where we saw moving figures and plenty of them. 'I had the "alarm" sounded just to remind those monkeys over there that they can't catch the Legion asleep, and the "regimental call" was blown on the off chance of its carrying to Ras-el-Chel and telling the company that there is business going on here."

"He sent us to put our trousers on then, and the Arabs gave us plenty of time to do it, for they didn't move until nearly seven o'clock, after we had been cursing them for hours for keeping us waiting.

"It was a good job for us that they didn't start earlier, for there were several hundreds of them with breech-loading rifles, and there would likely enough have been none of us left by daylight if they had had the sense to pour volleys into us before we could see well enough to pick them off. You see we hadn't enough ammunition on our side to waste it in volley firing.

"They climbed up into the palm-trees all round and shot down on us, but that gave us a better chance at them, for we couldn't miss birds of that size, and every shot we fired brought one of them down.

"Our bugler was the first to lose his number: he was shot through the head as he stood in the angle of the parapet and remained standing up as if he were still effective.

"This gave us an idea, and as each man fell afterwards we propped him up behind with a bayonet and stood him against the parapet. When the sergeant went out we stuck his pipe in his mouth, and he looked regular life-like, only more determined. Soon there was a row of dead men guarding the blockhouse, and they looked so calm and confident that the Oulad-Seghir evidently thought it would be too risky to come to close quarters with us, and gave up the attempt on the post in disgust, so that when our company came to our rescue at the double there was nothing for them to do.

"'Brave fellows, you have saved the post!' said our captain as he embraced the corporal and me, who were the only two left standing. But the worthy man was mistaken; it wasn't us that had saved the post, it was those others standing stiff there at the 'ready'—those others that he didn't embrace.

"The company marched past that line of dead defenders and sa-luted them, but the men were all laughing as they did it; they couldn't help laughing, for, my faith, those dead 'uns did look comical.

"That's how I got this bit of tin, *camarades*, and my friend Jules here ought to have got it, because he was one of those who actually put the finger-blight on the general's clothes and buried them."

CHAPTER 6

Two Tales of Desertion

Our evening "soup" on that Saturday was our first meal in Algeria, so this will be a convenient place to give general particulars as to the food of a legionary.

The daily ration given in kind, in Algeria, consisted of:—

Meat	300 grammes	(about 10 ozs.)
Bread	750	(" 25 ")
Coffee	16	(" 1/2 ")
Sugar	21	(" 2/3 ")

In addition to this issue in kind there was an allowance of eighteen centimes (nearly 2d.) a day for the provision of potatoes, vegetables, and wine—a quarter of a litre, or about half-a-pint, of which used to be issued about four times a week in my day.

There is a terrible monotony about the food, for every meal is very much the same and consists, except on rare occasions, of a dish called "soup" and bread. We would call this "soup" stew, and probably Irish stew, for it contains a lot of potatoes and vegetables. It is palatable enough and very nourishing, as a rule, but I am afraid that the regulated ten ounces of meat per man does not find its way into it. There is a lot of leakage both from the rations in kind and from the messing allowance, as most of the sergeants-major and the "*fourriers*," or company-quartermaster-sergeants, reckon to have some pickings from these sources. I found this out for myself when I became a sergeant-major, and I had serious trouble with my *fourrier* because he thought I was depriving him of some of his legitimate perquisites. Further than this, the cooks take toll of the food passing through their hands.

After allowing for all this, however, there is plenty left to satisfy a normal man in the climate of Algeria, and those who say that the

Legion is underfed are not telling the truth.

Personally, I cannot remember having ever eaten the whole of my ration of bread, and there were so many like me that there were men in my time who made a practice of collecting the uneaten bread and selling it to the natives, though to sell bread was an offence punished with eight days' imprisonment.

The only fault I ever found with the food was its want of variety, and that, it must be confessed, is a very serious fault.

A quarter of a litre, or about half-a-pint, of sweetened black coffee is brought to the legionary's bedside before he gets up in the morning, and with this some men take bread saved from the previous day's allowance; generally breaking it up and putting it into the coffee— making "slingers" of it, as the British soldier used to call the operation in the days before the present system of fancy messing came into vogue.

After this there was nothing till "morning soup" at half-past nine. The second, and final, meal of the day was "evening soup" at five, which was very much like the morning meal.

We didn't get much sleep that night. The wooden guard-bed and the single blanket that was our sole bed-covering were so occupied already with creatures that resented our intrusion that our first night in Algeria was passed in such terrible discomfort that on the following day we hedged against a repetition of it by taking in as much wine as our stomachs would hold, which certainly made us indifferent to the attacks of the insects and oblivious to the hardness of our couch; but in the morning I, at least, wished that I had put up with the insects, for I had a headache that made living very painful indeed—the horrible headache which always seizes the unseasoned indulger in the heavy wine of Algeria.

Our second day in Algeria, a Sunday, would have been a long wearisome day for us if it had not been for our two friends of the day before. They obligingly spent the whole day with us, drinking and smoking much at our expense, but giving us good value for what we spent on them in the shape of counsel and entertaining reminiscence.

Among the stories told by them was a tale of desertion, related by Jules, which I will try to reproduce faithfully:

"But yes, my friends, I have made the promenade," said Jules in answer to a question as to whether he had ever attempted to desert. "It would have been an adventure to laugh at if it hadn't been that the man most concerned in it took it too seriously.

"We were marching with a convoy to Mascara, and the commandant was a pig who not only marched us too much but fed us too little. We cursed him among ourselves day after day, but nothing came of the cursing until we were within a short march of Mascara. Then a German fellow named Goerth went from one to the other and suggested that we should go off on a march of our own and try our luck in getting to Tripoli. Goerth spoke as if it was the easiest of things, that getting to Tripoli, and it is likely enough that he didn't know any more than we did, that Tripoli was five hundred miles away.

"He got a dozen of us to agree to go with him, and as we were crossing a stream we hid among the oleanders on the bank until the convoy passed out of sight, none of our comrades giving the alarm, for it was no business of theirs.

"When we could no longer see the tail of the convoy we came out of our hiding-places and Goerth took command of us as if he was a sergeant and we his squad. He ordered us to form up and fix bayonets, and, when we had done this, he marched us off to a small Arab encampment that we could see in the distance.

"He told us as we went along that we would tie up the men and enjoy ourselves until the evening, when we would march on again and seek other opportunities of the same sort,

"This seemed to us to be a very good programme and we advanced gaily. As we approached the encampment we could hear the women shrieking with terror, as the Arab women always do when we of the Legion get to close quarters with them, and the men turned out to meet us. There were only about half-a-dozen men, and they did not look as if they wanted to fight, so we thought we were going to do what we wanted without hurting anybody.

"The *sheikh* came up to us in a very friendly fashion, and told us that he was an old *Turco* who had served under the tricolour for many years. He said that it was a great happiness to him to see some of his good friends of the Legion, and he hoped that we would come into his tent and give him the pleasure of entertaining us. He spoke so like a good comrade that he quite got over our leader, who ordered us to pile arms and follow the old man into his tent. Here we got a good meal of *couscous* and milk. All the time we were eating it the old *sheikh* "comraded" us till we came to think that he was a very fine fellow indeed. We ate till we could hold no more and then lit our pipes, feeling very comfortable and well disposed towards the *sheikh*.

"All went very happily until Goerth looked out of the tent and saw the Arabs taking away our rifles and bayonets. Calling on us to follow him he rushed out and took his rifle from the man who was carrying it away. But we were too comfortable to move, and nobody followed him out: we had eaten and drunk our fill, and our minds were not so set on Tripoli as they had been.

"Seeing that we did not come out, Goerth rushed back again, and, calling us a lot of filthy pigs and slandering our mothers, asked us if we intended to sit there and let the Arabs make prisoners of us.

"We told him that we didn't see why they shouldn't take us in; they had treated us very well, and it was the least we could do to let them get twenty-five *francs* each for us, seeing that we intended to go back any way.

"This made Goerth curse and threaten, but we took no notice of him.

"'They're not going to get twenty-five *francs* from me,' he said at last. 'If you lousy cowards won't go out and take those rifles back I'll blow my head off in front of your faces.'

"'That's your affair,' said one.

"'If you've got an idea that way get on with it; we don't mind,' said another.

"We of the Legion, you see, believe that a man's life is his own private property, and nobody would think of interfering with a comrade who had a fancy to end his engagement in the easiest way open to him.

"Goerth sat down facing us all, as we smoked there composedly, and took off one of his shoes. Then he put a cartridge into the rifle and, without saying another word to us, put the muzzle in his mouth and started groping for the trigger with his big toe.

"'A little higher, comrade, a little higher,' said one of us who was taking more interest in the affair than the rest.

"Goerth brought his toe higher and found the trigger. Then: *Puff! Crack!* and he was lying on his back with a hole as big as your fist in the top of his head. He *was* a fool, that fellow.

"Then the *sheikh* came in again, and he wasn't polite any more. He said several very rude things to us, so that we were sorry that we had let him have those rifles so easily; but it was too late to be sorry then. We were also sorry later, that we had let Goerth shoot himself, because he became a nuisance to us, owing to the Arabs making us carry him all the way into Mascara, where they got twenty-five *francs* for him as well as for us, which would have annoyed Goerth greatly if he could have known about it."

I tell this gruesome yarn just as it was told to me, as nearly as I can. I learned afterwards that Jules was actually one of a party which really deserted as stated.

Then, while we were on the subject, the man with the medal, whose name, if I recollect rightly, was Dubourg, told us another story which I verified later also.

When he was stationed at a post on the border of the desert, he said, three Germans belonging to the detachment disappeared. It was hardly believed at first that they could have deserted, for it was the height of summer, and it was difficult to realise that any sane man would have made off into the desert at such a time when death by thirst was almost a certainty, even if they escaped the bands of hostile Arabs known to be in the neighbourhood; but the fact that they had taken with them their arms, their kit, and their equipment, left no room for doubt.

Some days afterwards one of the runaways staggered back to the post, and going down on his belly at the first water he came to, drank greedily like a parched beast.

He was in a fearful state of exhaustion, and had cast away everything except his shirt, a pair of trousers, his rifle and his ammunition. He was taken before the officer commanding the detachment, who asked him sarcastically how he had enjoyed himself. Getting no reply to this question the lieutenant asked where were his comrades.

"One wouldn't come back, and I've put 'paid' to the account of the other," he replied.

Then he went on to tell how the three of them, suffering terrible tortures from thirst and not being able to go on any further, notwithstanding the fact that they had thrown away all but their rifles, had sat themselves down to consider their position. The "dirty" Prussian who had persuaded the other two—Bavarians—to desert by telling them that he could certainly lead them to Morocco, was asked what he had to say for himself, and then the man who had come back had coolly announced to him that he was going to shoot him. The other made no attempt to defend himself, and the Bavarian carried out his threat by shooting him in cold blood.

Some friendly Arabs were sent out to search for the other Bavarian, and found him almost at the last gasp. When he was brought in he confirmed all that the other man had said. The murderer was punished for the act of desertion only, it being held that he had justifiably killed the man who had led him astray.

Before we leave Oran let me tell the true story of the German prince who belonged to the Legion, a story which is set down in a recent book as a legend. It is nothing of the sort, for it is a fact that a member of the German royal house did serve in the Legion. His name, in the Legion, was Albert Friedrich Nordmann, and he died in the hospital at Geryville; of disease, not of wounds, as stated in the "legend." His body was brought to Oran, whence a man-of-war, with flag at half-mast, carried it to Germany. That is all—there was no romance about the service in the Legion of this cousin of William II.; no gallantry displayed in action, no Cross of the Legion of Honour taken by the general from his own breast, and no Chevaliers of the Legion of Honour escorting the corpse. I did not know him myself, I was not even in the same regiment, nor were we contemporaries, but I have met men who did know him, and they described him to me as a very ordinary young man, whose only striking characteristic was his standoffishness and reserve. I have never heard anything about his motives for joining the Legion, but imagine that he must have done something to seriously displease his august relatives.

By the mail boat that arrived on Monday there came a further batch of recruits for the Legion, and this lot were more fortunate than we were, inasmuch as they didn't have to sleep at Fort St. Therese at all.

They were now thirty-five of us, and of these twenty, including Petrovski and myself, were sent to Sidi-bel- Abbes and the other fifteen to Saida, where are the headquarters of the second regiment.

Among the new arrivals were two men, whose presence with us indicated that the age limits were not very strictly observed in recruiting for the Legion. One of them I put down, even then when he was clean shaven and had dark hair, as being nearer fifty than forty; and later, when he had grown a beard streaked with grey and the dye had worn out of his hair, leaving it very mouldy looking indeed, I gave him considerably over the half-century. The other one was a chubby boy without a hair on his face, or any sign of one, and he could certainly not have been more than sixteen.

Neither of these recruits could be expected to last long in the Legion if the life were one of such intolerable hardship as it has been represented to be, and the fact that they both lived to complete their engagements is, to my mind, fairly good evidence that service in the corps does not put a breaking strain on an ordinary constitution.

Sidi-bel-Abbes, the depot and headquarters of the First "Regiment of Strangers "is about as far from Oran as Dover is from London, but the West Algerian Company's trains could almost be beaten for speed by a bicycle ridden by a cripple, and the journey took us from early afternoon till late at night. In its early stages it was a very interesting journey to me. I had imagined that Algeria outside the towns was nothing else but sandy desert, and here I found myself moving leisurely through country dotted with white and yellow villages and country houses set in groves of citron, orange, date-palms, and fig-trees; and surrounded by vineyards and well-tilled fields.

It was my first introduction to the fact which I had opportunities of thoroughly digesting later on in other parts of Algeria, in Indo-China, and on the West Coast of Africa—that the French knock spots off the English in the matter of developing and beautifying colonies. We are taught at school that the English are the boss colonising nation that the world has ever seen, and this is, of course, true as far as the extent of colonial possessions goes, but the French know a great deal better than we do what to do with colonies when they get them.

At every station there was a crowd of black and brown natives anxious to sell green figs, oranges, grapes, tobacco, cigarettes and big luscious melons. They were evidently open to barter, too, for signs were made to me at three several stations to exchange a particularly gorgeous flowing silk tie—which I had bought at Marseilles to give myself a flavour of the gaudy south—for fruit, and similar overtures were made to others of our party for various articles, pocket knives being special articles of desire. None of our party, however, had need to barter, or to buy either, for Petrovski, with the thoughtless generosity that seemed to be natural to him, invited everyone to take whatever they fancied, and leave it to him to pay.

I begged him to limit his hospitality, for the men's own sakes, but he only laughed good naturedly and called me a regular old woman, while some of the men who could understand what I said looked at me as if I was trying to do them an injury.

I made a second attempt to stop the supply when I thought that they had taken as much as would leave them any loophole of escape from the fate of bad little boys who steal green apples; but my interference was taken in very bad part by the men, and received by Petrovski with laughter and a jocular "Don't be uneasy about us, granny." One of the Germans muttered that I was an uncomplimentary-adjec-

44

tived sheep's-head, while another ejaculated the German equivalent for "dog's-tail" three times with much disgust, and even the smiling Swiss's merry look seemed to come undone.

Then I shut up, and all the rest of the way chuckled grimly to myself and got much comfort in thinking of the sort of experiences they were going to go through to teach them the wisdom of my words of warning.

With the exception of the moody Austrian—who sat in a corner seat on the side opposite to the platform, and stared perseveringly out of the window—and myself, they all gorged themselves unceasingly, replenishing supplies at every station, so that by the time we reached our destination I knew from previous experience in Egypt that the Austrian and myself were the only two of the party who could have been unconscious of our interior economy.

CHAPTER 7

Knocked Down For Doing a Man a Good Turn

It was about nine o'clock when the train drew into the station at Sidi-bel-Abbes. A sergeant and two corporals were on the platform awaiting us, and without any loss of time they set about forming us up to march us to the barracks. They did not seem to be in the best of tempers, and there was some pushing and shoving on their part to get the men quickly into their places.

"Gently, my friend, gently," said Petrovski remonstratingly, as the sergeant pulled him somewhat roughly from the rear to the front rank.

"Silence, you dirty pig," said the non-commissioned officer brutally. "What do you think you have come here for? You'll find yourself somewhere where the birds won't trouble you if you don't look out."

My friend cast a furious look at the sergeant, and I was afraid that he would say or do something that would provide the non-commissioned officer, who looked and spoke like an out-and-out bully, with a peg to hang a serious charge upon; so, with great presence of mind, as I flattered myself, I diverted Petrovski's thoughts into a different channel by bringing my leg forward and kicking him on the shin with my heel as hard as I could.

He let out with a howl of pain, and, before I had any suspicion of what was coming, landed me a crack on the jaw that sent me sprawling.

"All right, old chap," said I laughing, somewhat ruefully, I must confess, as I scrambled to my feet, "I asked for it, and there's no harm done."

Poor Petrovski looked a trifle abashed. He had knocked me down on the spur of the moment, but had no sooner done so than he saw through my motive in kicking him.

"I'm sorry, my friend," he said, simply.

But the blustering sergeant was not for letting the thing pass so easily. He applied the most injurious epithets to both of us, and swore that he would put us in the guard-room as soon as we got back to barracks. As Petrovski was now on his guard he took all the abuse in silence, though I could see that he had hard work to restrain himself. As for me, I had been in the British army, and giving back-answers to superiors, no matter what the provocation, was no game of mine.

"My God!" said Petrovski, bitterly, to me as we marched side by side along the broad road that led to the barracks, "what humiliation and degradation we have let ourselves in for. Fancy being obliged to take everything that guttersnipes like that choose to fling at you, without having any chance to ram their cursed teeth down their ugly throats."

I saw that sympathy would do him harm, so I told him rather sharply that if he felt like that it was a sign that he had been let out of the nursery too soon, and he ought to have stayed at home until he grew up.

"Me!" he exclaimed, indignantly striking his breast with his fist. "Me! I have been an officer of the *Czar's* Guard since I was fifteen."

This was the first time that he had mentioned anything about his previous life, and he never referred to the subject again. It is probable that he regretted having been surprised into saying this much, for he was very reserved with me for some time afterwards. He was, and is still, a mystery to me, although he and I were on terms of affectionate intimacy for five years. What brought him to the Legion I can only conjecture. It certainly was not want of money, for, as I have already related, he had a good round sum in his possession when he enlisted, and he had regular remittances all the time he was serving.

I do not think that he was in the Legion on a woman's account either; he was too light-hearted for that. He did not appear to me to be stuffed with much military knowledge, and he was an execrable shot, but I am quite convinced, for all that, that he really was an officer in the Russian army, and not a disgraced one either. To this day I do not know his real name, but I identify him, in my own mind, with a certain Russian major-general who is said to have gained his knowledge of the French army at first hand.

Having heard much as to the brutal treatment of Russian soldiers by their officers, a scathing remark as to his disinclination to take medicine he had prescribed for others rose to my lips, but I restrained myself and merely said that everyone could see he was a soldier, a remark which seemed to please him.

Then I changed the subject by drawing his attention to sounds of *mandoline* or guitar playing that were floating in the air, saying that my first impressions of the town were more Spanish than Oriental. He agreed, but our impressions at first sight were considerably modified when we saw the town a little more, for Sidi-bel-Abbes is distinctly an Oriental town, but there is a Spanish flavour about it, and it is no unusual thing to see a *fandango* being danced in the streets.

When we got to the barracks it was after tattoo, which is at nine o'clock, and as the big parade ground was practically empty we escaped the chaff and rude remarks that usually assail a new party of recruits.

I rather expected to find the sergeant carrying out his threat to put Petrovski and myself in the guard-room for fighting, but he showed himself as being one of the barking but not biting sort and said nothing about it. This sort of non- commissioned officer gets very few men into trouble, but he does not get ready obedience, as men get to know that no bite is likely to follow his bark. The non-commissioned officer who is most dreaded by men of the Legion is the one who bites without any preliminary bark at all; this sort is very dangerous indeed. The non-commissioned officer most in favour is one who knows what he wants and never threatens without carrying his threats into effect. Men say they know where they are with a man like that, but they never can forecast what will happen to them when they are under the command of the other sorts.

Our names were called out in presence of an officer and then we were at once marched off to a barrack-room and left there for the night in charge of one of the corporals who had accompanied us from the station, who had a couple of old soldiers to assist him.

Personally I was very hungry, having had nothing but a couple of oranges since morning, and I had been confidently expecting a supper of some sort. Nothing was visible to my anxious eyes, however, and when the corporal started to undress himself and told us to look sharp and do the same as "Lights Out" was not far off, I philosophically took my hunger to bed with me.

The bed was simply a tick filled with straw, the exact counterpart of the bed of the British soldier in those days, and the bolster was also stuffed with straw, very tightly. I am told that there are iron bedsteads in French barrack-rooms now-a-days, (as at time of first publication), as there is a daily varied menu, but at the time I am writing of the bedstead was three planks laid upon two iron trestles which raised them about a foot from the ground. The bedclothing consisted of a sleeping-sack and two blankets; they have no use for sheets in the Legion.

The room was only used for the reception of recruits and therefore had fresh tenants every few days, so it was not surprising that I found more company in my sleeping-sack than I cared for. I dropped off asleep, however, in spite of them, and would no doubt have slept well had it not been for the night-long disturbances caused by the fruitarians. I was awoke by the flowery curses of the corporal, who had been woke up by a groaning recruit for the purpose of being asked the situation of a certain place the recruit badly wanted to find, and after that the night was filled with repressed repinings from the recruits, unrepressed curses from the corporal and the two old soldiers, and noises incidental to the hurried exits and leisurely returns of the afflicted ones.

It gave me an unholy feeling of satisfaction to see that Petrovski, who had taken the bed next to mine, was one of the worst sufferers, and I gave him no comfort when he dolefully whispered to me that he thought he had the black cholera. Instead of telling him that he had nothing worse than a big dose of concentrated essence of stomach-ache I informed him that I would not be at all surprised, and sympathetically added that it would be a bad job if it were so, for only about one *per cent,* of those attacked by black cholera recovered. What a pity it was, I continued, that he had not paid a little more attention to the advice given him by his "granny."

The man in the next bed to me on the other side heard my remarks upon the excessive mortality from black cholera, and as I spoke in French he understood them and they made him feel so much worse that he went and shook the poor corporal and begged him to send for the doctor, as he, and some others, would die unless something was done for them very quickly.

The corporal let out a few weird polyglot oaths, but apparently became convinced that something serious was the matter, for he got up, lit the lamp, and himself went for the doctor.

In about a quarter of an hour he returned with an officer whom I afterwards knew as Surgeon-Major Roux. The doctor came in hurriedly as if the corporal had been preparing him for a case of whole-sale poisoning, but it did not take him more than a minute or two to diagnose the case.

"I'll soon put you all right again, my children," said he good-hu-mouredly. "Come with me, corporal, and I'll give you a little of some-thing that will refresh them."

The corporal went with the doctor, and while he was away one of the unfortunates said that the proper remedy for the case was bran-dy, plenty of it, and no doubt that was what the doctor would send them.

I thought it possible myself that he would either give them brandy or opium, so I was as much surprised, though not as much disgusted, as any of them when the corporal returned with a big bottle of castor-oil and started serving it out in generous helpings.

Most of them declined, and some flatly refused, but they changed their minds when the corporal informed them that the doctor had said that it must either be castor-oil or eight days' *salle de police*.

I seldom saw any of that lot eating fruit afterwards.

This action on the part of the doctor may, at first sight, appear to bear out the hard things said of the medical officers of the Legion in a recent book, but I don't think that it was anything more than many English army doctors would have done in similar circumstances. I am quite unable to believe that a doctor of the Legion refused to give a suffering man on the march anything to relieve him, as stated in the book referred, to, and acted generally with such brutality as would be something like a disgrace to the medical profession. I was brought into close contact with three medical officers of the Legion—Surgeon-Majors Tanfin and Roux and Assistant Surgeon-Major Arragon—and I cannot imagine one of them acting in such a manner.

Men are certainly punished with eight days' room arrest—which is simply confinement to barracks with extra fatigue duty, but without punishment drill—for reporting themselves sick without reasonable cause; but this is a necessary provision for the prevention of shirking, and the same thing was punished by confinement to barracks in the British army in my time. It is quite possible, of course, for a really sick man to be punished in this way, owing to a doctor's mistake, but I never knew of a case. On the other hand I have known dozens of cases where men have gone sick and been excused duty for a day who have boasted afterwards that they only did it to get a rest.

CHAPTER 8

I Meet a Fellow Countryman

I was awakened in the morning by a voice shouting: "*Au jus. Au jus.*" (To the juice.)

Opening my eyes I saw one of the old soldiers carrying a large jug in his hand and going from bed to bed pouring about half-a-pint of hot coffee into each man's tin mug as it was held out to him. The coffee was not at all bad, though it was milkless and hardly sweetened enough, and it quickly roused me up.

Reveille was sounded a few minutes afterwards, and the corporal exhorted us to "Show a leg," "Come, out o' that," in words almost the equivalent to those that an English corporal would use in similar circumstances. It is the privilege of a French corporal to be the last man of his squad to get out of bed, so that all the time he was driving us he was still lying snug himself; and stayed so until we were all up and dressed.

"Where can I get a wash?" I asked the corporal, not having noticed a lavatory on the barrack-room landing as is the case in English barracks.

"Never mind washing just now," he said with a grin, as if it tickled him. "You are going to have a beautiful wash presently."

Unwashed and unkempt as we were—and I, and all those who had started out with starched white shirts, looked particularly disreputable—we were taken over to the regimental office, where we were inspected by the adjutant-major, the regimental staff-officer corresponding to the English adjutant, and then posted to companies, Petrovski and myself being fortunate enough to be sent to the same. From there we were taken to the bathhouse, where we got the beautiful wash promised by the corporal; it consisted in our standing in a row, quite naked, while half-a-dozen legionaries threw buckets of cold water over us. This amused the legionaries immensely, and many coarse remarks were bandied about at our expense—I can't say that I felt much entertained myself.

From there we were marched to the stores to draw our kits, and very good kits they were, too. First of all we were fitted with a pair of red trousers each. They were hardly a Pimlico fit even, for they contained enough material to make a pair and a half as trousers are worn in the British army, but there was a lot of chopping and changing before every one was satisfied. Then came a double-breasted black tunic with red facings and green epaulettes with red fringe; a blue greatcoat or *capote*, which is made so that the skirts can be buttoned back to leave the thighs free, and is always worn when on the march, usually directly over the shirt; a blue undress blouse or frock; a red *kepi* with the Legion's badge, a seven flamed grenade, in brass; two white canvas fatigue suits; two pairs of shoes, with the exact fitting of which great care was taken; a pair of black leather gaiters; two pairs of linen spats, such as are worn by our Highland regiments; shirts, towels, drawers; a knapsack very much like the pattern discarded in the British army forty years ago; a bag containing cleaning materials; and, lastly, a blue woollen cummerbund to wind round the waist.

This last is a most sensible article to provide for men who have to soldier in hot climates, for it does away with the necessity of wearing a cholera belt, and the support it gives to the back is a great comfort when marching. British soldiers serving in India and in Egypt often wear something of the sort, but the Government does not provide it.

Now what articles of an English soldier's kit are missing from the above list? Why, socks. They don't wear socks in the Legion. Some wear pieces of linen—called *chausettes Russes*, or Russian socks—wrapped round their feet, but the majority wear nothing at all between the bare feet and the leather.

When the kits had been issued we were told that there was an allowance of seventeen centimes a day, about a penny three-farthings, for the upkeep of underclothing and white suits, and that anything left of this allowance at the end of a quarter would be paid in cash after a reserve of thirty *francs* had been accumulated. There were very few legionaries who got any cash income from this source, but a few very careful men did manage to draw four or five shillings a quarter.

We were now allotted to our barrack-rooms and told to change into our drill suits at once and bring our civilian clothes to the company office when we had done so.

Petrovski and I were again drawn together, and with us in the same barrack-room were six other recruits, including the smiling Swiss, but not, I was glad to see, the unsociable Austrian.

The barrack-room we were sent to was a large one containing thirty beds, but there was nobody in it when we entered, the inhabitants being out at drill.

All the occupied beds had a card above them bearing the owner's rank, name and regimental number, with his kit neatly folded on the shelf, and the corporal who accompanied us told us to make ourselves at home on any of the beds not having these signs of being already bespoken. Petrovski and I took two adjoining ones, and at once set about changing.

When we had got into our white suits we took our plain clothes in our arms and went over to the company office together.

"Would you like me to sell your clothes for you," asked the sergeant-major. "I shall get a better price than you would, perhaps."

I replied that I would be glad to give the clothes to anyone who would take them off my hands, and Petrovski echoed me. We were not sacrificing much, for civilian clothes fetch next to nothing at Sidi-bel-Abbes, and ours, though of the best, would probably not have fetched more than five shillings.

In exchange for the clothes the sergeant-major gave us some good advice that would have been well worth the money to a military greenhorn, but I, at least, did not need it at all. The only thing he said that particularly interested me was a remark that he would keep his eye on us and see that the captain was not allowed to be blind to our merits if we happened to have any.

As we were talking to him the Austrian came in carrying his portmanteau, which he had stuck to until now. The sergeant-major made him the same offer that had been made to us, but the Austrian replied to the effect that he did not wish to sell his civilian clothing just then, and that he would be obliged if the sergeant-major would keep the portmanteau in the company store for the present.

"Want to keep your line of retreat open, eh?" said the non-commissioned officer banteringly. "No, my worthy man, that is not permitted. Legionaries are not allowed to have any articles of civilian clothing in their possession, so you will have to dispose of that truck today."

Then he told us to go over to the hospital, on the side of the barrack square facing the gate, and wait there until we were required to pass the doctor, so we heard no more of the conversation.

The medical examination was a mere matter of form; as far as I was concerned it consisted merely of the doctor asking me if I was all right and cautioning me to be careful in my dealings with the opposite sex.

When we returned to the barrack-room we found that the duty men had come in from drill and were hungrily waiting for the morning soup. There were two squads in the room, occupying separate ends, and two corporals. Each recruit was handed over to an old soldier, who was told off to show him how to pack his kit away on the shelf above his head, how to clean his arms and accoutrements and generally to act as a sort of dry-nurse to him.

The mentor who fell to my lot was a German named Swartz, a soldier of the first-class, who turned out to be a very decent fellow indeed. He and I got on famously together from the very start, for before we had got through the morning soup, which came up immediately, I discovered that he came from Cologne, and I was able to talk to him about his native place, having received much of my education at a place not far from there.

Petrovski was allotted to a Belgian named Dremel, who was a chum of Swartz, so we four formed quite a snug party.

Immediately after soup we were all, old soldiers as well as recruits, marched down to the cook-house to peel potatoes—another thing reminiscent of the British army, the only difference being that the French peel potatoes, and arrange the messing, by companies, while in the English army the rations are drawn and prepared for the cook-house by rooms. With all hands on the job, potato peeling never took more than a few minutes, but, short as was the time occupied, it was often a tight fit to get through with it before ten o'clock, when every company had to parade to hear the day's orders read.

After orders we recruits were taken over to the company stores again to receive our rifles, bayonets and accoutrements. We were told to spend the afternoon in getting these in good order, in readiness for a start at drill next morning; and the afternoon was not too long for the job, for my things, at any rate, appeared to have been in stores for some time and were sadly out of order.

There is no pipeclay in the Legion. All the belts and straps are of black leather, like those worn by our rifle regiments, and the getting them up is a slow and painful process, every part having to be heel-balled until it is as evenly polished as the heel of a new boot. Mine gave me a great deal of trouble, as I had never done anything of the sort before, and had declined Swartz' s offer to do it for me. I am afraid that when I laid the task aside as having been done satisfactorily my belts compared very unfavourably with those of the old soldiers, but the officers and non-commissioned officers are not hypercritical with recruits, and I soon got into the way of shining them so that they looked as well as anybody's. The *Gras* rifle, though it was very dirty and neglected, gave me no trouble at all, as I already knew pretty nearly all there was to know about firearms, and the way I set about cleaning it elicited commendation from the corporal.

"You're the right sort of 'blue'" he said, as he watched me. "You won't be in the awkward squad long. You seem to know as much about a rifle as a captain-instructor."

After evening soup Petrovski and I invited the whole of the twenty-six occupants of the room besides ourselves, and the two corporals, to adjourn to the canteen to wet our acquaintance. We did not meet with a single refusal; indeed I cannot remember meeting a teetotaller all the time I was in the Legion. I asked Swartz as to the propriety of inviting the corporals to come along, but was told that the proper way to stand treat to them was to stick a packet of cigarettes and a bottle of wine among their bedclothes.

The canteen was nothing more than a bare room with a zinc-covered counter or bar running along one side of it. Behind the counter was a comfortable-looking woman, who was neither young nor middle-aged, and not particularly good-looking. This was Madame la Cantinière, the modern survival of the dashing, handsome Cigarette of *Under Two Flags*.[1] It is impossible to fancy this up-to-date *vivandière* careering about on a high-spirited horse with a smart kepi perched roguishly over her ear. As a matter of fact she was knitting, and knitting as if she liked it. At her back were rows and rows of shelves filled with bottles and glasses.

About a dozen men were sitting and standing about, drinking and smoking, but they were doing both in a half-hearted sort of way, as if they were conscious that both wine and tobacco would have to be made to last a long time. The drink trade seemed to be in a state of stagnation.

When our lot trooped in *Madame* looked up hopefully, and then put down her knitting and advanced upon us with a gracious smile.

"You order what is necessary," said I to Swartz.

---

1. *Under Two Flags* by Ouida (Louise De La Ramee) also published by Leonaur.

"See, my friend, how much do you want to spend? "he asked. "Shall it be a litre and a packet of cigarettes to every two comrades? "

"No," said I magnificently, "let it be a litre and a packet to every man. And don't forget two bottles and two packets for the corporals.

"Bah!" interposed the pecunious Petrovski, throwing down a twenty *franc* piece. "Drink and tobacco *à volonté*—at pleasure—*madame*, if you please, to these good comrades as far as that will go. When that is down my comrade here—me—will give you another one."

As a pint of wine only cost something like a half-penny, or did in those days, in the canteen at Sidi-bel- Abbes, it did not require much calculation to forecast the state of that twenty-six men if they attempted to deal with that sixteen shilling piece: so, while the lady was serving the thirsty ones, I whispered to Petrovski that he was a blighting pestilence, and would be the cause of some of those men sleeping in the guard-room in their clothes for a few nights to come.

The irresponsible Russian's reply was a mere shrug of the shoulders and a disdainful look. He was not on very confidential terms with me just then.

English people do not associate drunkenness with the drinking of wine—red wine at any rate—and so it may not sound convincing to English ears to say that cheap wine is at the same time the greatest solace and the greatest curse of all troops serving in Algeria, not legionaries alone but soldiers of all arms.

The wine is good, very good, and the legionaries' appetite for it is only limited by their power of purchase. We read with something approaching awe of men who could make a practice of stowing away two or three bottles after dinner in the old drinking days, but a man who drank that quantity in the Legion would be counted a moderate drinker if he had money in his pocket to buy more and went away without it. I knew men in the Legion who could walk comfortably to bed with a quantity equivalent to six or seven bottles inside them.

I was hobnobbing quietly with Swartz when the sergeant-major of my company came in and beckoned to me.

"The sub-lieutenant wants to see you in the company office," he said, when I went over to him.

I drank up my glass of wine, told Petrovski and Swartz where I was going, and followed the sergeant-major out, wondering what the officer could want with me.

"What is the sub-lieutenant's name, *chef*"—the sergeant-major, I had learned already, is always addressed thus,—"and what does he want with me?" I asked as soon as we got outside.

He mentioned a family name well known in the Indian Army, and said that all he knew about it was that the officer had seen my name when looking over the company roll, and had asked him to send for me.

When I entered the office a smart young officer who was sitting on the corner of the table got up and looked at me curiously.

I saluted and stood at "attention."

"Are you Legionary Brown?" he asked in English.

"Yes, sir."

"Well, I'm glad to make your acquaintance," he said, holding out his hand with a smile. "We don't get many Englishmen here as far as I can see, and you're the only one in this company. Sit down and let us have a chat."

He then turned to the sergeant-major and told him not to let us interfere with his arrangements, and the non-commissioned officer sat down at his table and went on with some work he was doing.

The officer betrayed no curiosity about my past or my motives for joining, which was of course only the natural attitude of a gentleman, and our conversation was mainly about the Legion itself. I ventured to remark that he seemed to have got quick promotion, when he astonished me by saying that he had only been in the corps himself for about two months.

"Did you join as an officer, then?" I asked.

"Oh, yes," he replied. "It is not difficult for a man who has been an officer in a foreign army, and has left it for no cause reflecting on his honour, to get a direct commission in the Legion."

This was a revelation to me. I also might have joined as an officer perhaps if I had known the ropes, for I had been guilty of nothing else but folly, and had been honourably gazetted out of the British army. It was too late now, if for no other reason than that I had joined in a false name.

In the course of further conversation I learned the curious fact that I could not now get a commission unless I became a naturalised Frenchman, but that naturalisation was not insisted on in the case of those foreigners who got direct commissions. Furthermore, there were only two ways of getting a commission from the ranks. One was for gallantry in action and the other was by going through a course at the French military college of Saint-Maixent. This college is a French institution that might well be translated to England as a remedy for the increasing shortage of officers. Entrance to it is gained by success in an open competitive examination confined to non-commissioned officers, so that a commission in the French army can always be obtained by an ambitious non-commissioned officer who can prove his fitness for it.

Saint-Maixent is a sort of rankers' Sandhurst, and if the same plan were adopted in England, in conjunction with the granting of a living wage to junior officers, it would lead many superior young men who do not care to enlist under present conditions to adopt the army as a profession, and we should get a class of ranker officers quite as good as the Sandhurst-trained brand. That is the deliberate opinion of a Sandhurst man. At the present time promotion from the ranks in our army is practically non-existent for men without money or influence, commissions of the quartermaster class of course excepted.

We chatted on these subjects for the best part of an hour, and then the sub-lieutenant left me. The officers of the Legion do not come much into contact with their men on ordinary barrack duty, most of the military training being left to the non-commissioned officers, and I did not see much more of him, as he was transferred to another battalion soon afterwards. I rather think, though, that he put in a good word for me, as the captain took more interest in me for the short time I was in the company than was to have been expected if he had not heard anything about me.

When I got back to the canteen I found that the proceedings there had become pretty lively. The room was now crowded. There was a tuneful party in one corner singing a glee in German, a favourite pastime with legionaries of that nationality, a dense smoke-fog filled the room, there was a heavy winey odour in the air, groups of men were talking loudly in the language that came easiest to them, which seemed to be more often German than anything else, and bursts of boisterous laughter were frequent.

Everybody seemed to be light-hearted, carefree, and happy. What struck me most was the absence of coarse language, and I found that this unsoldierlike decency was the rule in the Legion, not because there were any regulations on the point, but simply because the men did not care for meaningless obscenity. Ordinary curses were pretty frequent and free, but they were such as did not outrage one's sense of decency.

The lady behind the bar was taking no money. Those who wanted anything went up to the counter and got it without giving anything in return, and the only indication that the *cantinière* was not giving it away was the fact that she tallied it on a slate as she served it.

Petrovski formed one of the group listening to an old legionary telling tales that kept his audience in roars of laughter. I joined the group round this raconteur, and was soon laughing like the rest at the witty and skilful relation of the comical situations brought about in the family of a probably mythical colonel of the Legion by his young mother-in-law falling in love with his soldier-servant. A capital farce could be made out of the story as it was told that evening in the Legion canteen; but it would have to be a French farce.

When the tale had come to an end Petrovski edged over to me and clapped me familiarly on the shoulder.

"Well, my dear granny, you were right about that money," he said good temperedly, "a twenty-*franc* piece goes a deuce of a long way here. I thought about what you said after you had gone, and sent out scouts to fetch some more fellows in, and now all this lot are helping to drink it."

'What do you say if we leave them to it and go out to have a look at the town?" I said.

He replied to the effect that it was a good idea, but suggested that we had better ask our two dry-nurses to come with us to show us round.

Swartz and Dremel were quite agreeable, so we four slipped away quietly, and in about a quarter-of-an-hour's time were dressed in correct walking-out uniform: red trousers, tunic, *kepi*, and sword-bayonet. When we got to the barrack-gate the sergeant of the guard stopped us to find fault with the appearance of Petrovski and myself, and there was a lot of smoothing out of wrinkles and tugging of belts into position before he would allow us to pass. This was all pure uncalled-for officiousness, because both of us were dressed as smartly as the clothes would admit of, and a great deal more so than three out of four of the legionaries we met in the streets afterwards. It must be admitted, though, that our appearance would have raised a broad smile or two at Aldershot.

We did not see much of the town that night, for after promenading aimlessly in the main streets in company with thousands of soldiers and civilians who seemed to be just walking about to kill time, Swartz lured us down a labyrinth of dismal side streets to take us somewhere where, he said, we could get something that was fit for a Christian to drink. When he said this I thought that he was out after beer, and readily consented, for I could have done with something in that line myself, even though it might have been nothing stronger than lager. But when he had landed us inside a low disreputable bar, in a part of the town that legionaries were not supposed to frequent, he called for a quarter of litre of "*Bapeli*" and four glasses.

I have tasted many weird drinks in my time—including trade gin distilled from sawdust, "Scotch" whiskey made in Germany from potatoes, rice spirit, and the native-made fire-water of Indo-China—but I have never come across anything so fiery as the liquor that was served in response to that demand. It literally scorched my throat and made my palate tingle as if I had taken a mouthful of red pepper. One gulp of it was enough for me, and less suited Petrovski, who spat it out as soon as he had tasted it. I never made a second attempt at drinking it, but I afterwards bought many and many a litre of it, as I discovered that it was capital stuff for hardening the feet, and, whenever I could get it, I always poured some into my boots, after I had got my feet into them, before starting on a march.

"Look here, my friend," said Petrovski to Swartz, "did you bring us here to have a little joke with us?"

"Don't you like it, then?" asked the German in a surprised tone. "Why, it's splendid stuff. You'll get nothing stronger anywhere."

' We are not looking for anything stronger," said Petrovski drily, "show us some place where they sell something about a quarter as strong; our stomachs don't happen to be armoured."

A couple of red-cloaked *spahis* and three or four legionaries, who were drinking the same stuff and apparently enjoying it, looked at us curiously and grinned patronisingly, as if they were thinking that the taste for the "splendid stuff" would come to us in good time.

"Come along," said Petrovski, "I've had enough of it. Let us go somewhere and get a bit of supper before we go back to barracks. I haven't got used to that soup yet."

Petrovski and I moved towards the door while Swartz and the Belgian moved towards the *bapeli* left in our glasses.

"It's curious that you didn't like that good stuff," said Swartz. "Both of you drink spirits when you are at home, I suppose, and there's nothing wrong with that stuff you've just left, I assure you. It's made out of good fresh figs, and it's the dearest thing to drink that you can get: it costs twenty centimes the quarter litre in that place, and twice as much in the *cafés*."

"Twopence for half-a-pint was indeed a high price for a legionary to pay for his drink, so *bapeli* was only possible on special occasions for those who were living on their pay, and poor Swartz' disappointment at our lack of appreciation of the special treat he had offered us can be imagined.

"I don't know where to take you to now," he said, lugubriously, when he followed us outside. "That twenty *centimes* was all I had, and I can't treat you anymore."

"Yes you can, my boy," said I, handing him a five *franc* piece; "only ask us what we'll have next time."

Petrovski saw my action, and handed a coin to his Belgian. 'You also may want to treat us, my friend," he said.

"Dart down here quick," said Swartz suddenly, as we were passing a dark narrow lane with mere hovels of houses on either side of it. "There's the picket just turning the corner in front."

"And why should we run from the picket?" I asked, as I tore after him.

"It is eight days if you are caught in this part of the town," he said.

"You're a cheerful person to select as a guide to innocent recruits," I remarked, when we had slowed down after satisfying ourselves that the picket was not taking any interest in our proceedings.

"Eh, but you would have come down here by yourselves, old comrade, and got caught by the picket for a certainty, if I hadn't brought you. What sort of a man is it, think you, who does not go at least once to a forbidden place? "

"He's right enough," laughed Petrovski. "Speaking for myself, I shall probably go there again, though I must say that I'm not particularly struck with the neighbourhood."

When we reached one of the principal streets and were passing a brilliantly lighted *café*—in the main thoroughfare, at any rate, Sidi-bel-Abbes is thoroughly French—Petrovski led the way inside.

The waiter looked askance at us, and asked what we wanted in a "don't want your custom" kind of tone, but when Petrovski began to order him about in his cool, dictatorial tone, the man's manner changed completely, and he became respectful to the verge of servility. I am coated, with humility myself, and I rather resented my friend speaking to that waiter as if he were a slave, so I tried to temper Petrovski's harshness by being myself very affable and asking for what I wanted in the style of one asking a favour.

The result was hardly satisfactory, inasmuch as the waiter completely ignored me, and Petrovski had to use his influence to get me a bottle of Bass that I had asked for four times in vain, after seeing the familiar red triangle hanging on the wall in a corner. I don't know why he should have been so disinclined to supply that bottle of beer, for they must have made a howling profit on it, seeing that it figured in the bill as half-a-crown's worth. I got my own back on that waiter though, for it fell to me to pay the bill, and I forgot to tip him, though he became amazingly civil when he discovered that the one who had been doing the ordering wasn't going to do the paying. There's a moral to this incident: it is that you are more likely to be kicked if you are humble and meek than if you are dictatorial.

There was another party of four legionaries in the cafe, and they appeared to be very much at home there. They were in the middle of what appeared to be a very elaborate dinner when we entered, and seemed to be very well-bred men if one might judge by their table manners and the tone in which they conversed. They never, from first to last, took the slightest notice of us.

"Do you know them?" I asked Swartz.

"They're *angehende corporale*," he replied.

"Probationary corporals, are they? "I said. "They seem to be doing themselves well."

"Yes," he said, "there's plenty of money in the probationary corporal section, and those four very likely dine here every night. You see there are a lot of swells in that section, and they get more money from home than the general run of us."

Then, in answer to my enquiries, he went on to tell me that there was a whole half-company of these sucking non-commissioned officers, and that they were selected generally from among those legionaries who had had previous military experience in other armies, and could speak French well.

"You've been a soldier before, I think," he continued—I had never mentioned it—"and as you speak German as well as French, you ought to stand a good chance of promotion if you show any smartness."

I was vain enough to think that the smartness would not be wanting, and already saw myself a member of that select half-company.

We stayed in the *café* so long that we had to double to get to barracks in time for tattoo; but the other party were still sitting leisurely over their coffee when we left. On my asking Swartz why they should not be in such a hurry as we were he told me that they had probably got leave to stay out of barracks till midnight, which any legionary who had been dismissed recruits' drill could get, though comparatively few applied for it except for nights when the Legion's band was playing in the town.

When we got back to the barrack-room we found most of our comrades feverishly engaged in cleaning their traps for the next morning's parade, making up for the time lost in the canteen, and their work went on long after lights-out, to the droning accompaniment of one of the legionaries telling stories, after the manner of the Arabian Nights, and this story-telling was still in progress when I dropped off to sleep.

CHAPTER 9

What a Regiment! What Men!

I was awakened next morning as on the morning before, by the cry of "*Au Jus*." Swartz had impressed upon me the advisability of being one of the first at the washhouse, as the accommodation was limited, and it was sometimes difficult to get a wash before parade, so I hopped out of bed at once without waiting to be hunted out by the corporal, and took my way downstairs the moment I had swallowed my coffee. I got a very satisfactory wash, and was grateful to Swartz for the tip, for most of the other recruits had to go on parade without any wash at all. After washing Swartz showed me the correct way to roll up my bed and fold the blankets neatly on top of it.

Then, after sweeping under my bed—a part of the room-cleaning that every man had to do, the remainder being done by the orderly-man, which duty had to be taken by everyone in turn—I was free to get ready for parade, and speedily wound my blue cummerbund round the waist of my white trousers, and put on my white jacket and cap. As the fall-in for parade always sounds a quarter of an hour after reveille, and as it is necessary to go down to the ground-floor to get a wash, it is a very busy time between reveille and the fall-in, and nobody gets ready much too soon.

We recruits of the last batch were formed into two squads with a probationary corporal in charge of each, and a corporal in command of the whole.

The barrack square is very little short of two acres in extent, and it was covered with men, probably as many as three thousand being on parade. There was not sufficient room for such a number to drill, of course, and I wondered what they were going to do. The point was soon settled by the battalions, and the different parties of recruits, with the exception of ours, marching out of the barrack-gate to the music of drums and fifes. We twenty were left behind and did our morning's drill in a corner of the square.

We were first of all put through the movements of extending from the right, left and centre, and then, when we could get ourselves into the proper positions at the word of command, we occupied the remainder of the time with a form of physical exercises, something like our "extension motions." We were kept at this, with a "stand-easy" of about five minutes in every half-hour, until about eight o'clock. All the commands and explanations were given in both French and German, a practice rendered necessary by the fact that most of the German recruits, even those from Alsace-Lorraine, did not understand French—and more than half of the legionaries are of German nationality, if those from the conquered provinces are reckoned as such. If asked, however, what their nationality is, most Alsatians insist that they are French, though their native places were taken from France forty years ago.

One of the recruits was a Levantine Greek, who understood neither French nor German, but the corporal was equal to explaining to him and giving him his native equivalents for the French words of command. It is astonishing what a number of extraordinary linguists there are in the Legion. Non-commissioned officers who can speak six languages are by no means rarities, and men who can converse in three tongues are to be found in almost every barrack-room. In that very company at the time I am writing of, there was a sergeant, a smart soldier, who was said to have been a professor of languages in a college in Switzerland. He was credited with knowing no fewer than twelve languages. He was certainly a master of those I spoke myself, and Petrovski told me that he had never heard a foreigner speak such good Russian, so it is likely enough that general report did not overrate his ability.

What struck me as being very wonderful was the fact that though a good percentage of recruits did not know any French at all when they joined, I never met, in all my time in the Legion, a man of six months' service who could not converse with ease in the sort of French that is spoken in the Legion barrack-rooms—which is not book French by any means.

At eight o'clock we were dismissed, and had nothing more to do, theoretically, till after morning soup; but in practice it worked differently. As we were trooping off to our barrack-rooms after being dismissed we were pounced upon by a sergeant and kept hard at it for the next hour and a half, going round the barracks with wheelbarrows and brooms doing scavenging work. This was our introduction to the hated *corvée*. Generally the fatigue work of the barracks is done by men sentenced to extra *corvée*, and by men undergoing room-arrest and *salle de police*, but all these men were now out at drill; and when there are no defaulters available, or there are not enough of them for the work to be done, the non-commissioned officers impress the first men they come across, and those who have not mastered the art of dodging get very little free time.

After "*La lecture du rapport*," or the reading of the orders of the day, we were kept at what is called "*Théorie*" until two o'clock. This instruction ranges from the pay and provision regulations, through the drill books, to musketry instruction and explanations of regulations of all sorts, and is continued into the trained soldier stage. As far as the instruction to recruits is concerned, military knowledge is relegated to second place, and the time is mostly taken up by explaining the different badges of rank and the proper compliments to be paid to each, and impressing the standing orders on the men's minds.

On this first day the "*Théorie*" was very interesting to me, because it included a visit to the museum, or "*Salle d'honneur*," as it is called, of the Legion. I read recently that this "Hall of Honour" is forbidden ground to the legionary. If this is so now, and I am very much inclined to doubt it, it was not the case in my time, for then every newly joined legionary was taken to visit it in order that he might be impressed by the feats of arms of his predecessors. It is difficult to believe that such a sure way of fostering *esprit de corps* should be abandoned, and I fancy that the statement must be a mistake.

The "Hall of Honour" is in a well-kept enclosure, walled off from the rest of the barracks, and is approached by a broad flight of steps. It is a very large room, with a painted ceiling, the work of a legionary, and the walls are literally covered with portraits of officers and men who have distinguished themselves, and with canvases of stirring scenes in the Legion's history.

The *adjudant-major*, who was acting as showman, drew our special attention to one of these pictures bearing the title "The Finish," and with soldierly feeling told us the story of the incident it commemorates surely one of the most gallant feats of arms that the world has ever known.

It happened in Mexico, where the Legion left the bones of nearly two thousand of its members. On the 30th April, 1863, 62 legionaries, with three officers, were acting as advance guard to a large convoy of provisions. They were attacked by a thousand Mexican cavalry, and fought their way to the *hacienda* of Camaron, where they barricaded themselves. The thousand cavalry were now joined by twelve hundred infantry, and the legionaries were confidently called upon to surrender. Captain Danjou, who had lost his hand in the Crimea and now wore an artificial one, refused to entertain the idea, and the Mexicans advanced to the attack.

Just think of it: two thousand two hundred men against sixty-five, and those sixty-five without a drop of water, although the heat was tropical. They defended themselves from eight o'clock in the morning until two o'clock in the afternoon, when a flag of truce again summoned them to surrender. Of the sixty-five there were but five now alive, and they were all desperately wounded. Who could expect men in their condition to stick out for terms? And yet they did stick out. "We will only surrender," said the non-commissioned officer, who commanded the wounded other four, "if we are allowed to march out with our arms, and keep them." The Mexican colonel granted these terms, but when he found that the garrison consisted only of five wounded men, only one of whom was able to walk, he made a remark that he had not been fighting against men, but against demons.

"This grand act of devotion was not in vain," concluded the *adjudant-major*, "for while the Third of the First was keeping that two thousand two hundred men employed the convoy got safely through. Soldiers of the Legion, remember the third company of this regiment and Camaron when it comes to your turn to fight."

In a glass case, under the picture, was the artificial hand of Captain Danjou.

Another picture to which our special attention was drawn, called "The Breach," illustrates an incident in Indo-China, where 390 legionaries gallantly held Tuyen-Quan against a Chinese army until a French brigade raised the siege thirty-two days afterwards. Of the 390 men in the place at the outset 190 were killed outright, and the majority of the others were wounded. The Chinese tried to take the place by assault no less than seven times, and on one of these occasions, commemorated in the picture, they blew up one of the most important of the defensive works with a mine, and a section of the Legion held the breach against them and prevented them getting in. A sergeant of the Legion acted as chief-engineer at Tuyen-Quan and constructed all the defensive works.

A whole book could be written round that museum of the Legion, and it would be a book well worth reading, too.

I was profoundly impressed by what I had seen, and I think that I was a much more valuable asset to France when I came out than when I went in. The finish to the *adjudant-major's* description of the Camaron fight looks, in print, a little unreal and theatrical, but in the actual delivery it was nothing of the sort. He was entitled to use that sort of language, for he had seen many stiff fights himself, and wore the Cross of the Legion of Honour.

"What a regiment! What men!" was Petrovski's remark to me as we trooped out of the "Hall of Honour" to resume the acquirement of such interesting facts as: "One red chevron denotes a soldier of the first class, two red chevrons distinguish a corporal, one gold chevron is a sergeant, two gold chevrons is the badge of a sergeant-major, an *adjudant* wears no chevrons, but carries a long sword like an officer," and so on.

From two till four we had foot drill, differing but little from our own infantry movements, and at four we were done for the day, with the exception of shining up for the morrow, and washing our white suits, which by this time were rather grimy, although we had only worn them one whole day.

Learning wisdom from our experience of the morning, Petrovski and I successfully dodged a sergeant on the look-out for someone to find work for in the hour that still remained until soup time; but most of the others were captured for *corvée*, and it seemed to grieve them very much, judging by the remarks they made when we saw them next, that we had escaped. It is a peculiar thing that men find misfortune easier to bear if their friends are unhappy also.

There are no washerwomen in the Legion. Every man has to do his own washing unless he cares to pay some other man to do it for him. We were quite able to find the small amount necessary to get our laundry work done by deputy, but we had decided that we would not shirk anything, so after soup we took our way to the "*lavabo*," a concreted basin formed in a running stream that passed through the barracks. All round the brink of this reservoir were men smoking, singing, and laughing while doing their washing, and I rather enjoyed the experience, which was not in the least like work.

There were only two or three out of our twenty who had not been drilled in some other army, and by the end of the first week most of us were sufficiently advanced to take our place in the ranks, had we been allowed to do so.

He would be a lazy man who could find anything to complain of in that first week's training, and I should much like to hear the opinion of such a man after he had served as a recruit in a British cavalry regiment for a week. I am betting he would regard the Legion recruit's course as a bed of ease by comparison.

The second week was a trifle harder, for we had now to march out to the drill ground of the Legion, which is some distance from barracks, and pass the morning in running drill. This training is undoubtedly trying to a man out of condition, and the blubbery ones were completely done up by the time we returned to barracks for morning soup. But it was splendid physical training, and as the breathing spaces of about five minutes came frequently and the pace was no faster than our "double," I cannot see that it could possibly do any healthy man the slightest injury.

The really hard part of the training was the marching. There was no mistake about that being a killing job. The legionary has not only to carry his personal kit when on the march—he has also to load himself up with his tents, little *tentes d'abri* like those used by our own troops when on the march in the abortive expedition for the relief of General Gordon, and the cooking pots. When fully loaded every man has seventy or eighty pounds' weight on his back, and he has to carry this for twenty, twenty-five, or even thirty miles a day under a burning sun, with a halt of ten minutes in every hour. We started training for this by marching short distances with nothing to carry but our arms, and gradually increased weight and distance until we were doing about twenty miles a day under campaigning conditions. When we had got to this stage I cursed the day I enlisted, and I fancy most of the others were doing the same; but the feeling of unbearable hardship got fainter with every march, and soon died away altogether.

CHAPTER 10

Volunteer for Tonkin

Sidi-bel-Abbes is a town of only about thirty thousand inhabitants, and Petrovski and I found life there very dull. We had seen all we wanted to see of the town before we had been there a week, and after that we only went out of barracks when we fancied a walk through the vineyards or a meal at a cafe, French or Arab, as the fancy took us.

"I've had enough of this," said Petrovski to me one day about three weeks after we had joined, as we were lying on our beds at "*siesta*" time—the summer programme had just commenced, and the time between ten and two was devoted to sleeping or keeping quiet in some other way, reveille being now at half-past four.

"I'm with you there," I replied. "I didn't come here for this dead-and-alive sort of life. I thought that there was always something moving here."

"Let's go to Tonkin," said Petrovski, just as if it was only a matter of buying tickets and going.

"Righto," said I chaffingly, "when shall we start—tomorrow?"

"We can't go tomorrow," he replied quite seriously, "but I fancy we might manage to start in a week or so. The sergeant-major told me this morning that there would be a draft going there within the next few weeks."

"We stand a healthy chance," said I. "We're not dismissed recruits' drill yet."

"I've got an idea that we can be dismissed recruits' drill tomorrow and get selected for the draft as well," he said in a bantering tone; "but you'll have to play the leading part because you can talk more convincingly than I can, and know more about military matters. You see by the notice-board that the colonel is tomorrow going to inspect all the recruits that had joined for the past month. Well, my idea is that you should tackle the colonel, tell him that you know a lot more about soldiering than he does, and that you enlisted to soldier, not to hang about in this hole and be taught things that you know a lot better than your teachers."

"It's awfully good of you to cast me for the speaking part," I said drily. "I suppose you'll be off the stage during the prison act, too. Sixty days is about the least I could expect for that little bit. How would you like sixty days of humping your kit in the sun for five hours a day, living on quarter rations, and passing the time when you weren't doing your heavy marching order drill in a dark and stinking cell. No, thanks, I've no fancy for conversing with colonels. I'll tackle the captain, if you like."

"The captain is no good," he replied; "the colonel is the man who can do the thing without asking anybody else, and if you are afraid to tackle him, I'm not. But I shan't be able to talk to him as well as you can, and I might fail where you would succeed."

"But where do you come in?" I objected. "A soldier in any army is not allowed to ask privileges for anybody but himself, you know."

"That's all right. You ask for yourself. I shall be next to you in the ranks, and I'll simply say 'me, too' to what you say."

"I might say something, but certainly not anything like what you suggest, if the colonel happens to speak to me," I said dubiously.

"Well, if you don't open your mouth I shall, and if I bungle myself into that sixty days, I shall think kindly of you when I am sweating under those marching order drills."

He was not stating any improbability when he said that he would very likely make a mess of it, for at that stage of his military career under the French flag he had not mastered the proper way to speak to an officer, and it was almost any odds against the colonel listening to him sympathetically. It was almost any odds against his listening to me, either, for what Petrovski wanted me to ask was something that the colonel had probably never been asked on an inspection parade before, and the natural thing for him to do, if he were in a good temper, would be to refer me to my captain, with whom I should have a bad time for going to the colonel over his head.

If the thing had to be done, and things that Petrovski set his mind on generally got done, I had much better do it than he, and so it was arranged between us.

My heart failed me, though, when Colonel Wattringue, commander of the Legion of Honour, and with a chest full of other decorations, stopped in front of me on parade next day. Luckily he made it easy for me by speaking first, or I don't think I should have carried out the arrangement. In Napoleon's days, we are told, the French common soldiers were allowed to write out petitions, or, more probably, got someone else to write them, and stick them on their bayonets, but that sort of thing doesn't go in these days.

When the colonel came to where I was standing shoulder to shoulder with Petrovski my captain said something to him that I did not catch, and the colonel stopped.

"What is your name, legionary?" he asked.

"Brown, *mon colonel*."

"The *Commandant de Recrutement* at Paris has written to me about you. You have served in the British army, is it not so?"

"Yes, *mon colonel*."

"Do you speak German?"

"I was educated in Germany, *mon colonel*."

"And what brought you here?"

"I thought to see some war service, *mon colonel*."

"That will happen, *mon enfant*," he said smiling.

"Will you send me to Tonkin with the next draft, *mon colonel*?" I blurted out. "I do not love this life in barracks."

"When you have nine months' service you may volunteer," he replied, and turned towards Petrovski as if to speak to him.

"Pardon, *mon colonel*," I said, and he turned to me again inquiringly.

"I am already a good shot, *mon colonel*," I continued, "and I can march like an old legionary"—which was not strictly true. "I have also been under fire many times. Could I not go with the next draft?"

"We shall see," he replied benevolently, as he again turned to Petrovski.

"My name is Petrovski, I also wish to go to Tonkin, and I, too, speak German, *mon colonel*," said the Russian in a breath, without giving the colonel time to open his mouth.

"I have heard of you, too," said the colonel. "You also have served, I am told. What brought you to the Legion?"

"I came to get the education of a man in the best school, *mon colonel*."

"Good!" said the colonel, looking pleased at the compliment. "Well, I cannot promise you anything, but I will keep my eye on you."

This was more satisfaction than we had any right to expect, but I was not sanguine of anything coming of it, and when, at the reading of the "*rapport*" next morning, we were astonished by hearing our two names and the Austrian's called out as having been posted to the probationary corporals' section, it seemed that our chances of going out with the next draft were quite extinguished.

The change, however, satisfied us for the time being, and we both set about our new duties in earnest. We had now done with recruits' drill—in fact we had to assist in instructing the recruits ourselves now, as well as making ourselves acquainted with the ordinary duties of a corporal and studying the "*Théorie*" books.

Our new comrades were generally reserved about their previous lives, but from their manners, and from unguarded expressions that they let drop now and again, it was evident that a good many of them had served as officers in other armies. Many of them were Frenchmen who had served a term as non-commissioned officers in ordinary French regiments, and one at least had been a commissioned officer in a French line regiment.

When we had been about a month at this work—a great part of my time being passed on the rifle-range assisting the musketry instructors—another surprise struck us at the reading out of "orders": our names, with a number of others, were called out as having been promoted to the rank of corporal, the Austrian again being one of the lucky ones.

I imagine that there was favour of some sort in this promotion, for we left many behind in the corporals' school who were there before us, and it may be that Petrovski's bold idea of tackling the colonel was responsible for it. At any rate he claimed the credit, and I didn't think that I was entitled to contradict him.

Our pay as corporals was twopence a day, four times as much as we had been getting as soldiers of the second-class, and twice as much as the pay of a soldier of the first-class.

In the same day's orders the expected call for volunteers for Indo-China was published, and an intimation given that no man might volunteer unless he had nine months' service, and had not suffered imprisonment during that time.

I hardly thought it worthwhile to ask for my name to be put down in face of this restriction; but Petrovski insisted that we ought to bring ourselves to the colonel's notice again, so we went to the sergeant-major, who, to our great surprise, took our names without demur, saying that the captain had told him to send in our names if we offered them. Although our names were down our chances did not look particularly rosy, for we learned that five times as many corporals as were required had put their names down. We were sent to the hospital for medical inspection, however, and augured from that that we were in the running. Another thing that made our chance look promising was the fact that we were not put in charge of squads, but were solely employed in assisting to knock recruits into shape.

CHAPTER 11

Embarkation for Tonkin

At last, a fortnight after we had given in our names, we were informed that we were among the chosen ones.

Our heavy clothing was now taken away and lighter garments, with a white helmet instead of the *kepi*, issued in its place; and, about a week afterwards, the draft, four or five hundred strong, paraded for departure, band and colours being formed up with us.

The colonel made a short speech of the "Soldiers, remember the glorious traditions of the Legion" order, while a crowd of the inhabitants stood outside looking through the railings; and then we swung out through the gates with the band at our head playing the stirring march of the Legion, the music being almost drowned by the rousing cheers of our comrades whom we were leaving behind.

Few of us came back to that barracks again probably more than half "settled down" for ever in the jungles, swamps, and burial grounds of Indo-China, while many more became so broken in health that they were discharged as being unfit for further service without returning to the Legion's headquarters.

When we got to Oran we were met by the band of the *Zouave* battalion stationed there, and marched straight down to the troopship, which had come in that day from Marseilles with other troops on board, and was waiting for us.

We had no sooner got on board than the ship cast off its moorings and moved away from the wharf to the accompaniment of the "*Marseillaise*," played by the *Zouaves'* band and sung by the troops on board.

What a rattling war-song is that same "*Marseillaise*"! We have nothing that comes anywhere near it as a patriotism-reviver, and I doubt if any other nation has either. Even we foreigners sang it with genuine enthusiasm, and, speaking personally, it has made my blood tingle many a time. I cannot fancy an Englishman getting enthusiastic over the *"Wacht am Rhein,"* nor a Frenchman or a German singing "Rule, Britannia" with fervour, but I have seen and heard men of almost every nation under the sun howl themselves hoarse over the *"Marseillaise."*

There were about seven hundred troops on board besides the Legion, and most of these belonged to the Marine Infantry. The French *Infanterie de la Marine,* by the way, is not a corps corresponding to our Royal Marine Light Infantry. The French regiments bearing this title do not serve on board ship—they are stationed at the French naval ports and in the colonies, and are no more marines, in our sense of the word, than any of our line battalions are.

On board the troopship we got better food than an English soldier at sea gets, and we were allowed half a litre (seven-eighths of a pint) of wine a day per man. For the rest, life on a French trooper is very much like life on an English one, and it does not, therefore, call for any detailed description.

When we were passing through the Suez Canal we had to tie up to the bank for a night, and sentries, all of the Marine Infantry, were posted round the ship's sides to stop any legionary who might take it into his head to desert. In spite of these precautions two German legionaries got clear away in some unexplained manner, and a third got half-way along one of the hawsers that held us to the bank. Having got so far he was taken with a severe attack of funk, and, not being able either to go forward or to come back, was constrained to call for help. He was evidently under the impression that we were in the River Nile, for when I, with many others, ran up to the bow in response to his frenzied screams he was yelling "Crocodile! Crocodile!" with all the power of his lungs.

As a matter of fact nothing could be seen that should have alarmed him, and there seemed to be no valid reason why he should not have got to the bank all right. But he was paralysed with terror except as to his voice and kept on screaming that he could hold on no longer. At last one of the sailors went down the hawser hand over hand, carrying the end of a rope, which he fastened round the legionary's body.

When the sailor got back on board again an order was yelled to the man on the hawser to let go. He couldn't make up his mind to do this for some time, till a lot of persuasive remarks of sorts had been addressed to him, and when he did let go he went splash into the waters of the canal, letting out an ear-splitting shriek as he did so. The sailor who held the end of the rope chuckled gleefully at this result of his mischievous slackening of the rope, and his hilarity became contagious when the poor beggar of a legionary was "accidentally" let fall into the water a couple more times before being finally hauled on board. This would-be deserter was put in the cells, where he remained for the rest of the voyage, expecting to be tried by court-martial at the other end, but he was released without further punishment when he landed.

I know something about Egypt, and I have often speculated as to the adventures of the two men who got away. It is pretty certain that they often wished themselves back on board the trooper before they got to their homes again—if they ever did.

The nearest French port was Pingeh, the port of Saigon, in Cambodia, but we had to make a call at Singapore to coal. As we were standing into the harbour I overheard two legionaries making it up to "hop the twig" there if they got a chance. My strict duty as a non-commissioned officer was, of course, to place them in arrest, and I afterwards wished that I had done so; but, both in the English army and the French, it was always a maxim of mine that an officer or a non-commissioned officer should never make any use of what he sees or hears by chance, except in very serious cases, and I did nothing.

We coaled from the wharf, so that anyone who wanted to desert had only to cross one of the gangways to be on English soil and free, as no country gives up deserters.

It seemed an easy enough thing to do, to get over that few feet of gangway, but the attempt cost one of the poor fellows I had overheard his life, and the other a severe wound.

All along the rail of the ship on the shore side were sentries of the Marine Infantry, and two sentries were on each gangway. All these sentries had their rifles loaded and their bayonets fixed, and their orders were to fire at any soldier who attempted to leave the ship, if they could not reach him with the bayonet; but on no account were they to fire upon or to pursue a man if he managed to reach the shore.

The legionaries, and the other troops as well, for all I know, were warned that these orders had been given, and were told to keep away from the shore side of the ship; but in spite of this caution the two men I have referred to made a simultaneous dash for freedom at different gangways, thinking, probably, that the sentries would not shoot to hit, even if they fired at all. If the sentries had been legionaries this belief would have been justified, for a legionary would never hit an escaping comrade if he could help it, though he would be sure to carry out his orders scrupulously by firing at him. The marine sentries, however, had no particularly kind feeling towards legionaries, for soldiers of the ordinary French regiments appear to think that "legionary" and "pig of a Prussian" are almost convertible terms, and they obeyed their orders to the letter.

The two Germans—it is safe to assume in nine cases out of ten, that a man who is trying to desert from the Legion is a German had seized a moment when the stream of coal-carrying *coolies* had ceased to flow from some cause or other, and the gangways were empty. The sentries at one gangway were taken unawares, and the would-be deserter was past them before either of them had guessed his intention. He was halfway down the gangway, and a few steps more would have carried him to safety, when one of the sentries brought his rifle rapidly to his shoulder, and, simultaneously, as it seemed, with the flash and the report, the poor fellow who was making a strike for liberty, pitched forward on his face, the top of his head being only a few inches from the free soil of the wharf, while the sentry who had fired at him was holding his jaw—he had been in such a hurry to fire that he had not taken time to jam the rifle-butt into his shoulder, and as the *Gras* rifle was a terrible kicker if held loosely, he got a crack on the jaw that made him use language so picturesque that there would be danger of its melting the type if I set it down here that is if it got so far as the printer, which I am by no means sure of.

While this was going on the second German had made a rush at the second gangway, but the sentries there saw him coming and brought their bayonets down to the "charge." He either did not notice that they had done this or could not stop himself in time, for he ran clean on to the point of one of the weapons and received a dangerous wound in the abdomen. He was taken to the sick-bay and transferred to the military hospital when we got to Saigon, but whether or no he eventually recovered I do not know, for I never heard of him again.

The other man was quite dead when taken up, having been shot through the heart, and his body was taken out to sea and cast overboard when we were beyond the three-mile limit.

This painful incident caused such bad blood between the legionaries and the marines that for the remainder of the voyage it was deemed advisable to keep them apart, and we were confined to one part of the ship while they were limited to the other.

When we got to Saigon we disembarked. The Marine Infantry draft went into barracks, for their regiment was stationed there, whilst the legionaries and some details for corps not at Saigon went into camp outside the town.

What we landed at Saigon for I have no idea. We did absolutely nothing while there, and after a week's idleness we embarked on the same ship again and were taken to the mouth of the Red River, so-called because the ferruginous soil of its basin colours the water a dark brown, where the ship threaded its way through a regular maze of fantastic-looking rocks, eventually coming to an anchor in a natural harbour. There was considerable speculation as to the meaning of our stopping here, for it was clearly not a part where troops would be disembarked, but our curiosity was soon satisfied by an order to get ready for transfer to river boats next morning. The next day two river gunboats, with three decks, like the *Lotus* and the *Water Lily* of our own Nile Expedition, came and took us off. After about six hours' steaming through the red muddy water we drew into a wharf and were formed up and marched ashore. This was the town of Haiphong.

We marched up a beautiful wide street lined with trees—the Avenue Paul Bert—to the barracks which were situated right at the end of it in a road named after General de Negrier. It was early evening when we arrived, and after we had been told off to barrack-rooms, in which the sole furniture was a long wooden guard-bed, we were allowed to go out into the town. Petrovski and I went out together in search of a decent meal, and found it in a cafe not a stone's throw from the barracks. Here we were waited on by a clean handy native, whose sex we could not agree upon. He, or she, had a rather pleasing face and wore a chignon, so Petrovski addressed it as "my dear" and proceeded to chuck it under the chin on the sly, which seemed to amuse it very much.

Noticing furtive smiles on the faces of two Europeans, presumably French officials, who were dining at the next table, I expressed the opinion that my friend was making a fool of himself, and suggested that it was a waiter and not a waitress. Petrovski scouted the idea, so we decided to ask, assuming that as our order had been given in French that language would be understood.

"Look here," said I politely, when the next course was brought, "my friend and I cannot agree whether you are a gentleman or a lady. Would you mind settling the dispute?"

"*Com biet*," replied the waiter imperturbably, at which the Europeans at the next table burst out laughing.

This struck both of us as being rather bad manners, and we looked our displeasure, at which one of the laughers bowed apologetically, and said:

"Pardon, gentlemen, we could not help laughing, because he said 'I don't know' in answer to your question as to whether he is a man or a woman. He is a man, of course, but that is no reflection on you, because all newcomers have some difficulty in distinguishing the sexes here. Men and women dress pretty much alike, they both wear *chignons*, and they both smoke or chew tobacco."

After that Petrovski guarded against further mistakes by treating all Annamites as men until the contrary was proved.

We had a very satisfactory dinner, winding up with coffee and liqueurs, and the cost was only about three shillings each. Thoroughly comfortable we strolled quietly back to barracks, when we met a rude shock. As soon as we put our heads inside the gate we were collared to take charge of piquets to go out and round up the bulk of our party, who were said to be painting the town a brilliant vermilion. The men had been making a first trial of *shum-shum*, a potent rice-spirit, and hundreds of them were riotously drunk. A fair number of them had to be carried to barracks and tied up when they got there to prevent them committing murder. It was midnight before we were at liberty to lie down, and it seemed to me that I had only just dropped off to sleep when reveille went. It was four o'clock in the morning, and by five we were on the steamers again on our way further up the river, with no idea of our ultimate destination.

It was a very depressing day. We were so crowded on the gunboats that we had not room to move about freely, and the only scenery was long stretches of mud on either hand. That afternoon we arrived at a miserable hole called Hai-Duong, and here we remained for a wretched fortnight, making practice marches through the rice swamps that surrounded it. These rice swamps are cut up into sections by dams or causeways about a foot wide. Along these causeways we had to tramp in single file for miles, the soft earth becoming slush when a few men had passed over it. It was therefore impossible for many men to follow the same track, so we had to move over the country in parallel lines of sections.

The only thing that broke the monotony of these abominable promenades was the frequent slipping and going flop, into the nine or ten inches of water that covered the rice, of some unfortunate or other, and these mishaps always caused more merriment than the incidents warranted. There was absolutely no excitement about these marches, for the country was perfectly quiet and there was no prospect whatever of shooting or being shot at. This sort of thing lasted until we were all so dissatisfied that the least thing would have caused a mutiny, but we got the order to move on before anything serious occurred. It was at Hai-Duong that some of our party felt like moneyed men.

There is a coin current in Tonkin called a *sabuk*. It is a little smaller than a farthing, and is made of some sort of brittle alloy. It has a square hole in the centre, so that it can be carried on a string or a piece of fibre. Our men discovered that seventy of these went to a penny, and many of them, for the mere pleasure of feeling that they had money and plenty of it in their pockets, turned all their French money into *sabuks*, until the place was denuded of the coin.

Our next halt was at a place called Seven Pagodas, and here we learned that we were on our way to join the second battalion of the 1st Regiment of the Legion.

The river scenery about here was a great improvement on that we had met with in the early part of the journey, as the shores were well covered with villages nestling among fruit trees and stately palms, with picturesque red-roofed pagodas showing here and there; but as we were all utterly sick of the dawdling journey scenery had no charms for us. The journey from Haiphong to Phu-lang-Thuong, the town we were bound for, could easily have been made in a single day, for the distance is only about sixty or seventy miles, and we were kept hanging about on the road for three weeks.

We got to our destination at last, and were split up among the companies of the battalion, Petrovski and I being posted to No. 1 Company.

It is unnecessary to load this narrative with history which everyone can read elsewhere if they desire to read it at all, but it is well that I should devote a few lines to the situation in Tonkin at this time in order that my story may be understood. As a consequence of the campaign of 1883-5, China had renounced all rights of sovereignty over the country, and Ham-Nghi, the Emperor of Annam, had been exiled to Algeria, his brother Than-Thai being placed on the throne under French protection.

But the country had never been properly subdued, and bands of Black Flags, or so-called pirates, had established themselves in the almost impassable forests of the Yen-The district, and were allowed to do pretty much as they liked up to the time of which I am writing, the back end of 1889. The French Government had now come to the conclusion that some energetic steps must be taken to put them down, but up to the time of my arrival in Tonkin there had been no organised expedition to the Yen-The district.

CHAPTER 12

A Narrow Escape

When I arrived at Phu-lang-Thuong the battalion of the Legion there was engaged in scouring the country in the vicinity, and it was in one of these reconnaissances under Lieutenant Meyer, of my company, that I saw the first shot fired in anger of the many I was to see during my service under the tricolour.

News had come in that a celebrated rebel leader named Doi Van was somewhere in the neighbourhood with a strong band, and several parties were sent out to look for him. It was the party I was with that found him. We were on our way back to our quarters, and were passing a *pagoda*, when the lieutenant spotted a body of men on some low ground a good way to our front. By way of encouraging the pirates to come on the lieutenant posted the bulk of us in the pagoda and went on with the remainder to a point where he was exposed to the view of the enemy. As soon as the pirates saw this handful of legionaries they thought that they had a soft job on, and started to round them up. Then the lieutenant ordered us to start for the *pagoda* at the run, as if we were badly scared.

The pirates, thinking that they had seen the whole force, advanced to the attack of the *pagoda*, led by a pretty and handsomely-dressed young woman on a horse. She was armed with a dainty Winchester carbine, and used it too, but she ran little risk from our bullets, as the lieutenant chivalrously ordered us not to fire in her direction. There were very few of us would have fired at her in any case.

Although the pirates outnumbered us by about ten to one, they did not stop long after they discovered that our party was not so weak as they had imagined, and though we followed them up when they drew off, we did not attain our object, which was the capture of their chief.

He was taken about a month afterwards, however, and executed. While he was lying in prison the young woman we had seen voluntarily surrendered herself and demanded to be executed with him. Her request was not granted—instead of being put to death, she was set free with no stain on her character, so to say.

The French authorities set great store on the capture of Doi Van. He had been a sergeant—*Doi* is the native translation of sergeant—of "Young Ladies," as the legionaries called the Tirailleurs Tonkinois, on account of their feminine appearance, and openly boasted that he had only joined the French service in order to study their military methods.

I had a narrow escape of being killed in this preliminary skirmish. I had bent my head while I was undoing a fresh packet of ammunition, so that my neck was not occupying the back part of the collar of my coat, and while I was in this position a bullet went in at one side of the collar and came out of the other. Had I been holding my head up at that moment it is a practical certainty that there would have been a vacancy for a corporal in No. 1 Company.

During the following summer the rebels became very enterprising, and even came down from their hiding-places and burned villages in actual sight of our barracks—but this was always done at night, and they took care to make off before troops could be got to the spot.

The principal man among the disaffected natives was one of the Emperor Ham-Nghi's *mandarins*, named De Nam. He was to all intents and purposes king of the Yen-The district, for three villages out of every four recognised him as the representative of the dethroned monarch, and all the villages, whether they recognised him or not, were obliged to pay taxes to him, in return for which he protected them from the demands of the regular Government tax-gatherers. The troops could not get at him, for his stronghold was in the depths of the forest, and the French did not know where it was situated. No information on this point could be got from the natives, not even from those who did not hold in with him, for his cruel treatment of those he suspected of being in league with the French had thoroughly terrified everyone who was possessed of useful information. I myself came upon some terribly gruesome evidence of this, which will be described in its proper place.

In the autumn of 1890, however, the French got some indications as to De Nam's stronghold, and it was decided that it should be found and destroyed.

The column sent out for this purpose was commanded by General Godin, but as it only numbered about seven hundred fighting men, it could hardly be called a general's command. On this column the Legion was represented by my company, about one hundred strong, under Captain Plessier.

On the night before we set out I was discussing matters with Petrovski. We were speaking in English, as we generally did when we were alone, as we leaned against the wall of the *pagoda* which served as a barrack. I had been saying that I would rather serve under our captain than under any other officer of the battalion, and remarked that if the Legion didn't do its fair share in the coming operations it wouldn't be his fault.

Petrovski agreed, adding that the company had probably been selected because it was recognised that we had the best officers.

"Thank you for your good opinion, my friends," said a voice from round the corner, in almost perfect English, and the captain himself stood before us. "I was not eavesdropping," he continued laughingly; "you were talking so loudly, and the night is so still that I could not help hearing you."

"You are an exception to the English proverb which says that listeners hear no good of themselves, *mon capitaine*," I said, as we stood at "attention."

"I am flattered by your compliment," he said, "particularly as you English *militaires* are such terribly severe critics. Do they still believe in England that one Englishman is as good as ten Frenchmen, eh?"

"No Englishman whose opinion would be of the slightest value ever did believe it," I retorted, a trifle huffily.

"No, of course not, my friend," he said laughingly. "It is only my little joke."

After some further conversation, which was mainly directed to Petrovski, he advised us to go to bed, and took his departure. This was the first intimation that I had of his speaking English, but he afterwards practised on me to a considerable extent by conversing with me on indifferent subjects at every opportunity,

Next morning we paraded as soon as it was light. The column had been divided into three sections, the first of which was composed of our company, and about a hundred native riflemen. The other two sections were made up of Marine Infantry, a Mountain Battery of Artillery, and more "Young Ladies." We took different routes, the general idea being that the first and second sections should meet at a place called Tin-Dao and proceed to attack the village of Cao-Thuong, while the third section would take up a position from whence the pirates' retreat could be cut off.

After a floundering march we met the second section, which the general accompanied, between six and seven in the morning. The general now ordered our section to take the lead and search the villages as we went along. After about two and a half hours' march, following the direction that had been indicated to us, we came upon the fortified village of Cao-Thuong, which was supposed to be the abiding-place of one of De Nam's principal bands. It was situated in a clearing of the dense forest, and covered a fair amount of ground, so we calculated at first sight that it must be giving shelter to at least a thousand men with their families.

We approached it carefully in skirmishing order, expecting every moment to hear the whistle of bullets, but we got right up to the palisade without seeing or hearing anything, and in a few minutes afterwards we were inside. The place was deserted. I looked round in wonder. I had been expecting to see interior defences in keeping with the bamboo palisade which showed outside, and here were fortifications that might have been made by a man who had been taught at the School of Military Engineering. I thought that we would have had some difficulty in getting into that village if the pirates had stood their ground; but the pirates turned out to have more military knowledge than even the sight of these defences would lead one to suppose, and they had a better card to play than staying in the village.

From the top of a mound in the village the roofs of what appeared to be some ruined houses were seen at about a hundred yards' distance, and the detachment of native riflemen belonging to our section of the column was dispatched to set them on fire.

We had now been on our feet, for something like seven hours, and the general ordered a rest. We had piled arms, thrown our knapsacks off, and were preparing to enjoy ourselves generally when a shower of bullets came hurtling among us. The artillery mules stampeded, and we snatched up our arms and knapsacks in quick time, without any more thought of resting. Presently the *tirailleurs* who had been sent to fire the houses came back and reported that the bush was so thick that it was almost impossible to get to the place, but that one or two of their men had cut their way through the thick undergrowth and found that the supposed ruined cluster of houses was in fact a strong fort filled with men.

Our section of the column was now ordered to attack it, while the artillery dropped shells into it over our heads.

"I'll bet you drinks and tobacco for the two squads that my squad gets there before yours," said Petrovski to me as we were forming up for the attack.

I accepted the bet, but pointed out that, seeing that the *tirailleurs* couldn't get there, it was extremely unlikely that either of our squads would arrive.

"We've got to find the way the people who are there got in," said Petrovski.

This, of course, was the obvious retort; but finding the way used by the garrison was not so easy as talking about finding it, and it would be questionable tactics to use it if found, for it would be sure to be strictly guarded.

Our captain's idea at first was that we should chop our way through the bush with the "*coupe-coupes*"—a sort of machete—that we carried for the purpose, but after we had been some time at this we discovered that it would take a whole day at least to cut a practicable path. The bullets came whistling through the foliage all about us as we worked, but did us no damage, as they all, without exception, passed over our heads.

When the hopelessness of attempting to get to close quarters with the fort on that side was recognised, the commandant of our section of the column ordered both the legionaries and the *tirailleurs* to leave that part and try the other side. We made but little headway here, also, for some time, but at last a narrow path was discovered and we advanced along it in single file. We found this path so overgrown, and the thicket on either side of it so dense, that we made but little progress.

The captain was in front, armed only with a *coupe-coupe*, and when we came in sight of the clearing in which the enemy had established himself, he stopped and ordered us to close up as much as possible, and rush out at the word of command. As soon, however, as the word was given, and we advanced to the attack at the run, we were received with such a heavy fire from tiers of loopholed walls that four of us went down at the moment of emerging into the open, and it was evident that before we could have got up to the walls the repeating Winchesters with which the pirates were armed would have made short work of the lot of us. Under the circumstances it would have been sheer madness to have gone on, for the greater part of our force was still struggling through the thicket, so the captain wisely gave the order for us to retreat to cover again.

I and another man of my squad were picking up one of my men who had been badly wounded when the man who was assisting me pitched heavily forward, emitting a drunken sort of hiccough, and nearly knocked me over. He had been shot through the head, and my squad had now two men to carry through the thicket instead of one. Far back in the thicket the "retire" was sounded, and we painfully bore our burdens back to our starting-point, where the *commandant* of our division formed us up to await the further orders of the general. We were directed to stay where we were until the artillery had pumped some more shell into the place. The Marine Infantry also poured volleys into the thicket from an elevated position in Cao-Thuong.

This firing seemed to be effective, for we could distinctly hear shrieks of pain after each discharge, and when it had been going on for about half-an-hour a voice from the thicket shouted something through a speaking-trumpet, which one of the *tirailleurs* interpreted as an intimation that we were killing women and children. This news was conveyed to the general, who ordered a temporary cessation of fire; but this was misunderstood by the pirates, for the megaphone voice was heard jeeringly asking if we had used up all our ammunition, and offering to supply us with some if we would come and fetch it. This was followed by a terrific fire from the pirates, as if they wished to show us that they had so much ammunition that they did not mind wasting it.

It was now late afternoon. The heat all day had been stifling, and we had been on the go since four o'clock in the morning, carrying our heavy knapsacks. Moreover, we had had nothing to eat. We of the Legion were all seasoned men, and the native riflemen were hardy and unburdened, but the raw youths of the Marine Infantry were absolutely incapable of making any further effort. It was hardly to be wondered at, then, that the general decided that the further attack must be postponed until the following day. We accordingly took up our quarters in Cao-Thuong for the night. As soon as the pirates realised that we were not going to trouble them further for the present, they ceased firing.

We of the Legion had a sumptuous meal of fried pork, one of us having found a small pig in the course of the operations, and after this I was detailed to superintend the grave-digging party.

When the man of my squad who had been killed came to be searched a letter addressed to me was found upon him, and, sewn up in a flannel belt which he wore round his waist, there were six British war medals. These were surprising finds, for I had never heard the man speak English, nor had I ever been at all friendly with him. I had once heard him talking about India, and judged from his peculiar intonation, his appearance, and the dark markings at the base of his fingernails, that he was a half-caste from Pondicherry, the French possession in India. He was a very quiet, reserved man, who seemed to make no friends, which must have been choice on his part, for he was rather popular in a general way with the men of the squad.

The letter was a long one, so, after just glancing at it, I put it in my pocket to read when I had more time. When I did come to read it I could not keep my eyes dry. It commenced by apologising for troubling me, and went on to say that it was written under the influence of a feeling that he would not come out of the operations alive. Would I, it continued, in the event of his forebodings being justified, be so kind to a fellow-Englishman as to send the medals which would be found upon him to his younger brother in India, whose address he gave. These medals, he explained, were those won by his grandfather and his father, both officers of the British Army, and he himself had enlisted in the Foreign Legion in the hope of adding to the collection—his mixed birth rendering him ineligible for the European regiments of the British Army. His mother, he said, although a native of India, was actually married to his father, and the medals were given to him by his father on his deathbed.

To me this was a most pathetic document. Reading between the lines I could imagine the poor fellow shrinking from telling me his story when he was alive, and even refraining from letting me know that he spoke English, because he was afraid that I would treat him with the tolerant contempt which the European generally bestows upon the Eurasian. There was also his touching reference to himself as a fellow-Englishman—he wanted to be on a level with the men who had won the Maharajpore, Gwalior, Crimean, Turkish, Mutiny, and Ashantee decorations that he had inherited. What a terrible wrong men who make mixed marriages do to their children!

I showed this letter to the captain, who exclaimed, "Poor fellow! poor fellow!" as he read it. He gave me the medals and also a letter from himself to send to the brother, an Indian railway *employé*. That letter ought to have made the recipient proud of the dead man, for in it the captain said that he had never met a better soldier, and I supplemented this by a pious lie to the effect that he would probably have got the Cross of the Legion of Honour if he had lived.

CHAPTER 13

Reconnoitring a Pirate Stronghold

Next morning we advanced to the attack again, but when we got to the stronghold it was empty—the pirates had decamped in the night, leaving not a corpse nor a single wounded person behind. That they must have had many both killed and wounded was evident from the quantity of blood about the place. I very much doubt if we could have taken the position even if we could have made our way to it easily, for the ruined village had been turned into a regular fortress—a company of Royal Engineers could hardly have made a better job of it. An opinion was prevalent among the French to the effect that the pirates had skilled European assistance, and there was some talk among the legionaries of a mysterious "Sir Collins," presumably an Englishman, who had been turned out of the country.

If any Englishman was there I do not suppose for a moment that he was there to help the pirates to build fortifications, and "Sir Collins," if he had any existence outside the imagination, was probably what the Anglo-Indian calls a "T.G."—travelling gentleman. It was well known that the pirates received useful assistance sometimes from Chinese regulars, so the more probable explanation of the fortifications is that some Chinese military officer who had been educated in Europe was responsible for the instruction of the pirates in military engineering.

While the first and second divisions of our column were occupied at Cao-Thuong, the third division, which had been posted to intercept the fugitives, had been rather severely handled, and had utterly failed to prevent the pirates' retreat. This division rejoined us three days after the fight, and then the whole column scoured the country for three days, when the legionaries of the column with a company of native riflemen were detached to form a new post on the site of a former one that had been abandoned owing to its extreme unhealthiness. This new post was named Nha-Nam, and our captain was placed in command of it.

It was about half-a-dozen miles from Cao- Thuong, and the district was supposed to have been rid of the pirates by the recent operations; but so far from this being the case we soon found that we were in a regular nest of hornets. We had first of all to build a fort, for there was very little left of the previous post except a couple of *pagodas* that had been incorporated into it. While this was going on we were attacked regularly every night, and very often in the daytime also. Building operations under these conditions were very irksome, for after passing a sleepless night we were in no good fettle for a hard day's work, but in three weeks' time we had made our position secure enough to warrant our taking the offensive. It was supposed that De Nam's principal stronghold was somewhere in the neighbourhood of Hu-Thuong, the position at Cao-Thuong being now recognised to have been a mere outpost, and on the 9th December we left Nha-Nam in force to look for it.

We reached and passed through the village of Hu-Thuong without anything happening. When we were a short distance beyond the village, the keen eyes of our scouts detected a masked path leading into the bush. We were ordered to follow this path. It was just like a burrow cut through the wood, and it was evident that we were on the right road to the place we were looking for, for such trouble would not have been taken to cut a road like this unless it led to a post of importance. It was early morning, and the sun was not at its full power, but in the path the air was close and stifling and we were bathed in perspiration as we toiled along.

"Come along, *mes enfants*," said the captain cheerfully; "some of you will be late for the ball if you don't hurry up."

"I wish I'd never taken a ticket for the adjectived entertainment," growled a German behind me. "Thunder and lightning! couldn't I do a few *schoppens* of cool lager just now."

"I hope this isn't going to be an all-day job like Cao-Thuong," said another. "I believe in regular meals myself, and if they'd only arrange the fighting so that it would come between morning and evening 'soup' I could give 'em better value for their money than they get by making me scrap on an empty stomach."

"Pig!" said another man good-humouredly, "you are always thinking of your stomach. Just keep your eyes open for another swine today, will you? that one you found at Cao-Thuong was jolly fine."

With such chaff as this we stumbled on until we came to a clearing, when the captain ordered us to rush out, but not to fire until we were fired upon, as we might not have been seen, and there was a chance in this event of getting the whole lot of us into the open before hostilities commenced.

The pirates were apparently waiting for us, however, for the first man had no sooner emerged into the clearing than the *rat-tat* of Winchester repeaters told us that the fight had commenced.

I fancy that though we had seen nobody and heard nothing since entering the path, we must have been observed by some pirate outpost sentries, who probably did not fire upon us in the hope that if left alone we might not discover the stronghold after all.

We could see nothing but high palisades, and thought at first that we had only to get through these to be amongst the enemy, but when we rushed up to the obstruction and could see through the interstices we found that we had taken on a bigger job than anyone had dreamed of. Inside there were a series of trenches, one behind the other, which were afterwards found to have sharp bamboo stakes sticking up from their bottoms, and beyond them was a stretch of staked ground backed by another palisade, above which could be seen the parapets and bastions of a fortress of great extent. These works stood on ground much lower than that on which we were standing, so the tops could not be seen above the first palisade as we approached it.

We were protected from a frontal fire to some extent by the palisade, but were enfiladed from loopholed palisades running almost at right angles to us as we stood. These loopholed palisades covered trench communication between the principal fort and a subsidiary one situated to the north of it. We started hacking and tearing at the palisades for all we were worth, but as it was apparent that even if we got through the handful of men of which our force consisted would have no chance of taking such a strong position, the captain ordered us back to the higher ground with a view to finding positions from which we could successfully return the enemy's fire and get some useful idea of the extent of the stronghold and the character of its defences.

The native *tirailleurs* had already opened fire upon the pirates who had been annoying us, and we moved round to assist them. As we lay concealed behind folds in the ground and tree-trunks, firing away at any mark that presented itself, the natives on our side kept up a jeering conversation with the enemy, who were well within hearing distance. As they spoke in the vernacular I could not understand what they were saying, but I imagine that many unkind personalities were indulged in, inasmuch as both native riflemen and pirates seemed to be worked up to demoniacal fury at times when a lull in the firing permitted the cross-recriminations to be distinctly heard and appreciated.

I was afterwards told, though, by a native sergeant who could speak French, that though each side did make slighting remarks about the female relatives and the ancestors of the other, and referred to the enjoyment they would have when they came to make a meal of their adversaries' livers, the bulk of the conversation had reference to the comparative merits of service under De Nam and under the French, each side trying to persuade the other to desert.

It was very slow work, according to my idea, and I took the opportunity offered by the captain being in my neighbourhood to suggest that I and a few men might be better employed in making an examination of the other side of the fort. He asked me if I could make a rough military sketch of the ground, and on my replying in the affirmative, he told me to take another corporal and two men and try to make a circuit of the enclosure in which the fort stood, jotting down such particulars as would be likely to assist any future attack. Assuming that I had neither paper nor pencil, he offered me his field note-book, but I produced the necessary articles, which I was never without.

"You had better go that way," he said, pointing to the south. "I shall probably move round the other way myself directly to attack the gate."

"Who is to go with me, *mon capitaine?*" I asked. "May I take Corporal Petrovski and two men of my own section?"

He replied to the effect that I might take any corporal junior to myself and any two men, and I went in search of the Russian, whom I had not seen since we left the road to enter on the path. I found him at the other end of the line, and he didn't want at first to come with me, because he wanted, he said, to bag a pirate who was firing at some distance apart from the others, and seemed to be trying his utmost to bag my friend, and had got so near to succeeding that he had sent a bullet through Petrovski's helmet.

Having collected my two men we crept along under the palisades, I pacing the distance while the others went on in front of me keeping their eyes and ears open. At eighty paces from our start the palisades made a turn, and progress became difficult owing to the palisades on that side being placed right on the edge of the forest, which rendered that part practically safe from attack, and accounted for the defenders having congregated on the other side.

After we had gone about a dozen paces in this direction I was able, by peeping through the palisades, to see the ground between the first and second rows, as the second row was not continued round this side, but came up and joined the first row. Behind the second row there was a long stretch of turf, perhaps twenty feet wide, and then came ground so thickly planted with pointed bamboo stakes that it would have been an absolute impossibility for any number of assailants to have got through them before being shot down from the walls of the stronghold, which I could now see plainly in all their length. At the far end from where I stood, that is at the spot where our men were engaged, was a half-moon work, evidently covering the entrance, and at the corner nearest to me, and about a dozen yards from where I stood, was a bastion upon which there was a group of men clad in a dark green uniform. This was, no doubt, a piquet posted to watch that side; but they were all looking in the direction of the firing, and were not even keeping under cover, so it was very evident that they had no suspicion of our presence. They were a fine mark for a volley, but no good purpose would have been served by shooting them, and the firing would, moreover, have attracted attention to us and put an end to our exploring mission.

I motioned to the others to proceed with caution, and we made our way as noiselessly as the difficulties of the path would permit for another fifty paces, when we found on peeping through the palisades again that we were opposite to another bastion, also garrisoned by men who were looking the other way. This was the other corner of the fort, and the palisade here took another turn. We had rounded this, and I was taking a look through the palisade and noting the points for my report, when there were sounds behind us as if someone was forcing a way through the undergrowth. We had no time to hide, so just dropped on our knees with our rifles at the "ready," and waited for the appearance of the foe, who was in force, if one was to judge by the amount of noise he made. Over on the other side the firing was hotter than ever, but now it was broken by cheers as if some of our men were trying to take a position by assault while covered by the rifle fire of the remainder.

"Now then," I whispered as the noise of snapping twigs came nearer. "You take the first one, Petrovski, and so on till the fourth comes to me. Then we'll let 'em have a volley if there's any of 'em left."

All at once the noise ceased as if the advancing enemy had become aware of our presence, and then it recommenced, but now receding as if they were beating a rapid retreat. As the noise got fainter and fainter I peeped to see if it had aroused the attention of the men on the bastion, but they were still looking in the direction of the firing.

Then I laughed quietly at a thought that came into my head.

"What's the joke?" asked Petrovski.

"I was laughing at the idea of four legionaries being scared by a herd of wild pigs," I said.

"I think you're right, corporal," said one of the others, grinning. "I fancy I heard 'em grunting."

But Petrovski wouldn't have the wild pig idea at any price, and for anything I know to the contrary he may have been right; but wild pigs seemed to be the likeliest explanation.

We now went for ninety paces in the new direction, when we came to another bastion on which we could see no men at all, and a few steps further on our progress was barred by a stream, staked on the bottom and with an impenetrable thicket on the other side of it. I had now ascertained that the fort was about seventy-five yards long by about forty-five yards wide, that the walls were about ten feet high, and that there were bastions at three corners and a half-moon work at the other. It was pretty nearly impregnable on three sides, and on the fourth it was so well protected that it was extremely improbable that any force without artillery could force an entrance. I now gave the word to return.

We had no sooner turned to retrace our steps than I heard a rustling among the treetops and casting my eyes in the direction of the sound I saw a man ensconced on a small platform at the summit of a tall palm. He was trying to attract the attention of someone inside the fort, and I had no doubt that he wished to make our presence known. It was the usual practice of sentries posted in trees like this one to shout out their news through a sort of megaphone, but this one apparently thought that he was in a sufficiently dangerous position as it was, and did not want to make it a certainty that he would be discovered by us. If he had had any sense he would have laid low on his perch until we had passed along, for the news of our being there would have been just as useful to the people inside when we were a bit further away as it would have been then.

I am no believer in purposeless killing in war, but it was out of the question to leave him there to signal our exact whereabouts and our doings, so I brought my rifle to my shoulder, and he came tumbling down with a crash until he reached the tops of the lower trees, where he stopped. The people in the fort now commenced to fire at random and kept it up as if they believed there was an extensive force attacking that side, but though bullets were whistling around our heads all the way back not one of us was hit.

When we rejoined the company and I had made my report the captain ordered the "cease fire" to be sounded, and then directed the troops to withdraw along the path we had used in approaching. We were not allowed to depart in peace, however, for all the way back to the road we were exposed to a heavy fire from the enemy's scouts, who seemed to be moving along a path parallel to ours, though we could not see them, and could only reply to their shots by firing at random into the bush.

My company lost two killed and four wounded in this skirmish, which was a very small sacrifice of life to make for the valuable military information we had gained. We had located beyond doubt the principal stronghold of the pirates, and got such information about its construction and size as would be of the greatest value when it came to be attacked by a proper force.

Our discovery, however, brought disaster upon sundry innocent people. We had hit upon the place almost by chance; but the pirates did not believe this. Two days after our reconnaissance a Major Tane led a column composed of Marine Infantry and native troops against the stronghold, but he either did not pay any attention to the information we had collected or did not have it, for he had to retreat with very heavy loss. At the captain's request I had written out a report of what I had seen, and when I took it to him he made the remark, which was certainly justified by what we had seen, that the taking of the fort was more of a job for the artillery than for infantry—so it is hardly likely that he was consulted before the disastrous expedition was sent out two days later. We did not have any hand in that expedition, so I can say nothing about its details—I only mention the expedition at all to introduce what follows.

On the night of the day following this abortive expedition I was corporal of the piquet at the post of Nha-Nam, and observed a red flare in the sky as if there was a big fire in progress not far away. This was reported to the captain, who took no action on it that night. The next day, however, he led us in that direction to make our usual daily reconnaissance, and I saw the most horrible sight that had ever offended my eyes.

We were making for a village called Lang-Han, and when we were still some considerable distance from it we came across two rows of human heads, one row on either side of the road, stuck up as if they had been placed there as a sort of mocking guard of honour. On the faces of all there were looks of agony that caused those heads to haunt me for many a long day. Further along, on the slopes of a little hill, some little distance from the village, the ground was strewn with dismembered, disembowelled, and unmentionably mutilated trunks of men and women, and arms and legs which looked as if they had been literally torn from the bodies to which they had belonged. This human debris bore marks of fiendish torture inflicted during life, tortures which cannot even be indicated in print, and the general effect was so indescribably nauseating that several of us strong men were made physically sick by it.

Going on to the village we found other corpses, some of them half-burnt; but these were whole, as if the killing had been done in fight.

We learned afterwards that the pirates had jumped to the conclusion that we had been told the whereabouts of their stronghold by a Spanish missionary priest, and they had gone to a village a couple of miles or so from our post, where the priest lived, to seize him. He got wind of their coming, however, and fled to Lang-Han; but the pirates followed him there, killed him and such of the inhabitants as resisted, set the village on fire, and, taking some couple of dozen men and women villagers prisoners, had driven them to the little hill to torture the life out of them. De Nam's second in command had a horrible reputation for fiendish cruelty, and it was he who was said to have been responsible for this atrocity.

A day or two after seeing this gruesome sight, I was corporal of the guard, and on going my rounds just as day was breaking, one of the sentries drew my attention to a flag-like object stuck in the ground at a little distance from the post. I, in my turn, reported this, and was told to take a couple of men and inspect the object at close quarters.

I found it to be a piece of bloodstained cotton cloth, which seemed to have once formed part of the uniform of a *tirailleur*, and to the bamboo pole supporting it was attached a letter written in the native character. I couldn't read this, but one of our lieutenants translated it, and found it to be a proclamation, in the name of the Emperor Ham-Nghi, issued by a pirate leader named De Tham, who had united his forces with those of De Nam.

This document was rather long, and its object was to point out to the French officers that they were not playing the game in trying to drive De Nam, De Tham and Company away from their forest strongholds, and begging us to depart and leave them to carry on their ordinary avocations in peace.

As these avocations included the stealing of women and children to sell them to the Chinese, and the wholesale smuggling of opium, to say nothing of their short and summary methods with villages that would not pay taxes to them, the letter or proclamation seems to have been a somewhat *naïve* production.

At any rate the effect it had was not what the pirate chief might be supposed to have expected. So far from the Frenchmen going and leaving the poor pirates in peace, detachments of troops began to arrive from many garrisons with a view to worrying them more than ever.

This new expedition started out from Nha-Nam on December 22nd, between eight and nine in the morning. It consisted of about 450 Europeans, for the most part belonging to the Marine Infantry, and 300 natives. There was only half of our company employed, and we were detailed to guard the artillery, so it looked as if we were not destined to see any close fighting on this occasion. We got into the path that led to the stronghold without meeting with any opposition whatever, and were at once ordered to set about cutting down the bush to make a road. This looked to be a pretty stiff job, for the vegetation was so thick on the ground that it would have been quite impossible for a man to force his way through it. The trees, too, grew so closely together that it was very dim and twilighty in the path, and in the half-darkness our coupe-coupes looked miserably inefficient tools for the work in hand.

We set about chopping and hacking, however, with such hearty goodwill that by twelve o'clock we had got about a hundred and fifty yards of good wide path available, and had made a platform for the five mountain guns we had brought with us. It was very hard work, and at mid-day we were all utterly exhausted, so the colonel in command gave the order for us to cease work and rest for half-an- hour. The enemy, very considerately, did not interfere with us during this much-needed interval, but we had no sooner restarted our clearing operations than a heavy fire was opened on us from both our left and our right front . Several men were hit at the first discharge, and for a moment it looked as if we were going to stampede like a lot of frightened sheep .The artillery, however, opened fire and saved the situation, though the firing could hardly have done much damage, as the shells were in most cases stopped by the dense bush.

A half-company of *tirailleurs* was ordered to try to take the detached redoubt belonging to the pirates, but when it emerged into the open space in front of the fortifications it was received with such a deadly fire that it retreated in quick time.

Then a few legionaries, some Marine Infantry, and another half company of Tonkinois, were sent to reinforce the attacking party, and another attempt was ordered.

It was now two o'clock, and high time that we should be making some headway if we were to achieve any success on that day. The word to advance was no sooner given, then, than we rushed at the job as if we wanted to get it over. We dashed through the stream which stood between us and the redoubt, regardless of the fact that its bottom was thickly set with pointed stakes, but when we had got that far we had to cross a flat piece of ground that was swept by the enemy's fire, and then get through the palisades before we could come to close quarters at all. We got within about a couple of dozen yards of the defences, but the enemy's fire was so hot and so well sustained that we went down like ninepins and had to retire in a hurry and take shelter from the bullets by getting into the stream.

Further reinforcements were sent to us, and we got the order to try again.

Back again we rushed, bayonets at the "charge" and a man toppling over at every step. This time we actually got near enough to make thrusts at the pirates through the loopholes they were firing from. Next to me in this final rush was the lieutenant commanding the half-company of Tonkinois which originally formed the storming party, and as our powder-blacked faces were close together as we ran he shouted cheerfully that we looked like winning the race and being first in.

When we had got up, and he was emptying his revolver into the loopholes whilst I was making lunges into them with the bayonet, a bullet coming from my right passed so close to me that it actually tore a hole through the bottom of my jumper. I thought for the moment that I was hit, and then I saw the lieutenant drop to the ground—it afterwards transpired that he was shot through both thighs, and it was probably the bullet that gave me such a narrow squeak that found him. The fire from the Winchester repeaters of the rebels was terrific, and it was quite evident that we would never get near enough in such numbers as would make a successful assault probable, so instead of leaving the lieutenant where he fell, as would have been necessary if there had been any chance of getting in, I went to his assistance. A sub-lieutenant of Marine Infantry did the same, and we both bent over him at the same moment.

"Never mind me, my friends, my account is made up," said the lieutenant as we started to examine him roughly to see the extent of the damage. "I expected this. It was on this day in 1870 that my father was killed at Bourget."

I got a stretcher party, and as we were lifting the wounded officer on to the stretcher a strange thing happened: a bugle in the pirates' redoubt sounded the "Cease Fire," and a pirate got up on the top of their wall and shouted through a megaphone that they would not open fire again until we had removed all our dead and wounded. It was, in fact, only when we made another movement to assault half-an-hour afterwards that the pirates opened fire on us and drove us back with heavier loss than ever.

While we were thus employed several different parties were assaulting the main fortress in different places, but not one of them got in. Petrovski was with one of these parties, and succeeded in getting right up to the walls, through the two palisades and across the ground sown with sharp stakes and man-traps, but here he fell on to a sharp bamboo stake which passed through his body, and it was with the greatest difficulty that he got back again.

The pirates now began to take the offensive, for other bands had come up and were making a diversion in our rear, and as we seemed to be on the edge of a disaster the colonel gave the order for us to retire. Including the officer mentioned above, we lost 9 killed and 24 seriously wounded in this skirmish.

This was the third attempt we had made on this stronghold, and the pirates had every reason to be satisfied with the result in each case. It must be remembered that these men were really better armed than we were, for the bulk of them, thanks to the enterprise of English and American gun-runners, were in possession of Spencer repeaters, while the majority of us were only armed with the old *Gras* rifle, the *Lebel* rifle having at that date only been issued to the Marine Infantry.

Further, they were fighting behind fortifications that would have been a credit to any military engineer, and as far as courage was concerned they could fairly claim to be second to none in the world. All the same, we felt bitterly humiliated by these successive failures, and hoped that the next attempt would be made under better considered conditions. Our repulses were due to the fact that the French officers persistently refused to recognise the military ability of these pirate commanders, and consistently underestimated the fighting power of their men.

These operations were a great assistance to us of the Nha-Nam garrison, for all the newcomers had to take a hand in the brickmaking, the bamboo-cutting and carrying, the navvying, and the general work incident to the construction of the post. This gave us a spell of relief for which we were very thankful.

Four nights after the attack the pirates again came to within five hundred yards of the gate of the Nha-Nam post and left another long letter on a flagged pole as before. It leaked out that this letter was, like the other, a long-winded argument about the injustice of the French proceedings, and offering not to molest them in other parts of Tonkin and Annam if they would leave the pirates in peaceable possession of the Yen-The district.

CHAPTER 14

Poor Petrovski

It was decided to send the wounded down to the hospital at Phu-lang-Thuong, a distance of about twenty-four miles south, and my squad, together with a section of native *tirailleurs*, was detailed to act as escort. I was very glad that this duty had fallen on me, because my friend Petrovski was one of the wounded going down, and I was rather concerned about his state, for his wound was a very ugly one, the bamboo stake having penetrated the abdomen. My selection appeared to be an act of kindness on the part of our captain, who never missed a chance of doing kind little actions of that sort.

When our little column was lined up for the start it seemed to me that it presented a very vulnerable appearance. First came the "point"—one man of the *tirailleurs*—then, after the "point," at a distance of about fifty yards, the "cover point" of four men and a corporal. After these at a similar interval came the long line of sick and wounded in bamboo stretchers carried by *coolies* and escorted by the remainder of the *tirailleurs*. Behind the sick toddled the wives of the *tirailleurs*, carrying a pole over the shoulder, from the front of which depended the family cooking-pot, which balanced the larder and the husband's kit at the rear.

My squad of legionaries came last of all, we having been detailed to act as rearguard because it was thought that if the column happened to be attacked at all the attack would be sure to come from the rear.

A Tirailleur Tonkinois looks a very comical figure until one gets used to him. He wears a *chignon*, on the top of which is perched a lacquered hat very much like a dinner plate in shape. This is fastened on by red ribbons which pass round the top of the hat and under the chignon, the effect at first sight being very ludicrous indeed. It is beneath the dignity of these warriors to carry anything beyond their arms and ammunition, so our column presented the strange spectacle of natives of the country loafing along at their ease while we Europeans were loaded up like pedlars' asses.

As regards their fighting capabilities these native riflemen are a very mixed lot. Those of them who belong to the hill tribes reminded me very forcibly of the Ghurkas of our Indian Army, and are excellent soldiers in every way, but the natives of the low-lying delta are mere dummies, of no more military value than a Bengali *baboo*.

They are all very companionable though, and some of them know enough French to carry on a conversation. One of them with this escort spoke fluent Spanish, which was something of a mystery until it came out that he had lived for many years with a Spanish missionary priest. Another one of those with us on this journey appeared to have had some dealings with the priesthood, too, and seemed to fancy himself more than a bit as a linguist; but the only justification for this was his ability to say "*Ora pro nobis*." This phrase did duty for everything. If anyone said "Good morning, Johnny," to him in French, the answer, with a grin, was "*Ora pro nobis*"; if he was asked chaffingly how he got on with his wife the same reply came, accompanied by the same grin; and to the numerous fancy questions that were fired at him to provoke our risible faculties he never failed to give us our laugh by dealing out the same three words with the air of being extremely well satisfied with his erudition.

The rear-guard were supposed to march some eighty or a hundred yards behind the women, but the ladies evidently preferred our company to their own, and no matter how much we hunted them on they would always drop back again until they were just in front of us. We couldn't understand what they said, and our remarks were Greek to them; but when we addressed any remark to them they would smile and show their beautiful black teeth, throwing back some repartee that caused intense amusement to the other women, and would probably have amused us also if only we could have understood it.

They rushed back on us in a panic once. It was in the first hour of the march and we were passing through a belt of forest at the time. When we looked to see the cause of their alarm we saw that a magnificent tiger was leisurely crossing the road in front of them and apparently taking no notice of them at all. Tigers were fairly plentiful about those parts—some little time before this a sergeant-major of the Marine Infantry was eaten by one as he was passing from one post to another.

That night we put up at a native village. There was no sign of life as we approached it, and the lieutenant of *tirailleurs* who was in command of the convoy halted us and ordered me to take my squad and reconnoitre. When we got close up we found the heavy ironwood gates fast closed, and there was no response when I hammered on them with the butt of my rifle. The village was surrounded by an earthen rampart about six or seven feet high, the top of this being thickly set with bamboo and prickly pear so as to form a hedge that could only be got through by chopping it down, while at the foot of the rampart there was a stagnant ditch edged with bamboo palisades. I went back to the officer and reported. Then he gave me the order to force a way in and open the gates from the inside.

It didn't take us long to chop a passage through the palisade and the hedge with our *coupe-coupes* and lift out of their sockets the heavy wooden beams which fastened the gate. We didn't see any living thing, nor did I come across any sign of life either, when, in obedience to a further order, I searched the village through from end to end. Everything was in good order, but there were no inhabitants. Whether they had fled from their homes through fear of us, or to avoid the attentions of De Nam, De Tham & Co., I don't know; but I think it likely that they had been scared by the horrible treatment meted out by the pirates to that other village after our discovery of the stronghold of Hou-Thué.

Inside the defences the houses were all huddled together in such a way that there was hardly room for two men to walk abreast between them, and the interiors of the dwellings were largely made up of narrow crooked passages. No doubt the village was built in this way to make the defence of the houses easy if an enemy should happen to force a way into the village, and the means were admirably adapted to the end.

When the sick had been made comfortable in the houses I went to see how Petrovski was getting on. I found him in a high fever and in great pain, but quite cheerful and inclined to joke. I didn't feel at all cheerful, for I was very fond of Petrovski, and I didn't think that we would get him as far as the hospital, for it was plain to me that peritonitis had set in, and that he hadn't a hundred to one chance of life. I asked permission to sit up with him, but the lieutenant said that he wanted me to command the night piquet. He gave me permission, however, to look in on the sick man as often as my duty would permit, and this enabled me to perform many little services for my poor friend.

We had not covered more than seven or eight miles on the first day's march, but we made somewhat better time on the second day, as the road was now a wide embankment running through the rice fields. It was not soft like most of these embankments, but was a properly made road which looked as if it had been existence for centuries. The second night was passed in a *pagoda* which the French call by the name of a gallant legionary who gave up his life here to save his comrades when the Chinese were fighting the French for the possession of Tonkin. I sat with Petrovski for the greater part of this night, but he was delirious most of the time and gabbled in some language not known to me. In the morning before the start I found him quite conscious, but very feverish and weak, and in answer to my enquiry he said that he felt almost free from pain and was in two minds as to whether he would not get up and walk the rest of the distance.

Although he said this jokingly he must have known that he was in a very serious state, for as I silently pressed his hand he asked me, in quite a matter-of-fact kind of way, to see that some letters, which he had enclosed in a packet addressed to me, were forwarded to the addresses on them if anything happened to him.

I was not able to get near him during the march, for my position in the column was far removed from his, and all through that day it seemed to me that the monotonous cry of the bearers, which translated would be, "Oh, mother! oh, mother" was Petrovski's dirge.

He was still alive, however, when we got to the hospital at Phu-lang-Thuong, but he was unconscious when I managed to get a look at him after he had been put to bed. I worried the doctor on duty to tell me of his chances, but the officer only shook his head and shrugged his shoulders by way of telling me gently that in his opinion there was no hope. Next morning at daybreak I was on my way back to rejoin my company, never expecting to see the big-hearted Russian again.

We did the return journey in one day, and were back at Nha-Nam in time for evening "soup," which is only a figure of speech in Tonkin, for the messing there was very varied.

105

CHAPTER 15

Stronghold Captured at Last

Next morning I was sent out to take my share in the hard work of preparing for the general assault on the pirate stronghold.

These preparations consisted in clearing away the forest so that the guns could play freely on the enemy's fort. And what a forest it was! Try to fancy geraniums, fuchsias, and such like flowers, thirty feet high and with trunks twice the thickness of a man's body. Imagine, multiplied a hundred thousand times, the scent of an old-fashioned flower garden thickly planted with stocks, wallflowers, pinks, mignonette, carnations, and any other sweet-smelling flowers that come into your mind. Picture gigantic flower-trees whose blossoms start the day a pure white and then change from this successively to the palest of pale pinks, and every other shade in the gradations of red until at sunset the flowers are a deep rich crimson. Palms, bananas, magnolias, *frangipannis, shaddocks*, and every other tropical tree that you can call to mind, with a great many others that you never heard of, were to be found there, covered with ivy and climbing plants of all descriptions until the whole was one glorious tangle of scent and colour.

And the inhabitants of these virgin forests! Gorgeous peacocks, pleasing silver-pheasants, flocks of screaming parrots and parakeets, deer, wild pig, bears, panthers, tigers—were all to be found there in plenty, practically unmolested.

Working parties chopped away at the undergrowth under the protection of squads of their comrades fully armed and on the alert. As soon as a space was cleared a temporary fort was made to hold it, and the men garrisoning these forts got what sleep they could as they sat down with their arms in their hands. Lookout platforms were fixed in the tops of tall palm-trees, which were ascended by means of primitive ladders formed by joining thick bamboos on to one another and

106

passing short lengths of bamboo through holes so that there was a foothold on each side of the pole as it was fastened upright against the tree-trunk. Officers or non-commissioned officers, generally the latter, kept watch on these platforms day and night for any thread of smoke appearing above the trees, any sudden flight of birds, or any other sight or sound that might give an indication of the whereabouts of the enemy.

I had a most weird experience in one of these observation points one night. The heavy scent of the flowering trees as it came up to me seemed to narcotise me, and the gentle swaying of the tree-top emphasised its effects. I fell asleep. I was awakened by a blow in the face, and, starting up without realising where I was, I withdrew my arm from the branch I was holding on to, and only just managed to grab the edge of the platform as I was rolling off it. I was horribly frightened, and it was some little time before I could pull myself together sufficiently to regain my former position.

When I had recovered myself I looked round to see where the blow in the face had come from, and found that I was absolutely alone at the top of the tree. What it was that struck me I do not know to this day. The obvious explanation is that a bat or a bird flew against my face, but I doubt if that is explanation sufficient to account for the black eye I found myself possessed of next morning, which could hardly have been caused by a bat or a bird. I think it more likely that I was struck by a spent bullet, and this view is somewhat supported by what followed—though I must admit that if it is the correct explanation the incident borders on the marvellous.

In order to get rid of the heavy feeling that still clung to me, and get the sickly flower-scent out of my nostrils, I lit a *cheroot* and smoked away while trying to put a meaning to the various noises that floated up to me from below. Presently I heard the far-off report of a rifle and strained my eyes in the direction I judged it to come from, with a view to seeing the flash if it should happen to be repeated. I saw no flash, but the report came again and again. If I could see nothing I could report nothing, I thought, and I was making up my mind that the firing was too far away to concern me further when there was a whizz and part of a leaf fell into my lap—the sportsman, whoever he was, was evidently sniping at me, and I began to wish that I was somewhere else.

I quickly threw away my cigar and unslung my rifle to return the compliment as soon as I could locate him, but though he kept pep-

A LEGION SNIPER

pering away for another half-hour never a flash could I see nor any indication that would enable me to return his fire. The piquet down below seemed now to have become aware of the sniping, for I saw a party go out on the stalk. I heard next morning that they had located the shooter, but he didn't stop long enough to give them a look in. There was no more firing that night, but I was very glad, all the same, when the time came for me to be relieved.

At last, on the 9th of January, Colonel Frey, who was in command, gave the word "Go!" and we made a general assault on the stronghold, but didn't succeed in getting in. Next morning the artillery peppered the fort until the buildings in the interior were set on fire, and on the morning of the 11th we assaulted again. This time we did get in, but there was no enemy there to receive us; he had decamped into the dense forest at the back during the night, and had carried all his killed and wounded with him. It was impossible for our commander to have prevented this manoeuvre, as we couldn't get round to the other side of the fort in sufficient numbers. Inside the fort was a regular village which had been knocked all to smithereens by our artillery fire, and, taking it all round, I think that the honours of this brief campaign rested with the pirates, for they had stuck to their post as long as any troops in the world could have stuck to it, and had then faded away almost before our eyes without leaving us anything to boast of.

We scoured the country in all directions during the next few days, but could find no traces of them, so the authorities came to the conclusion that they had dispersed and made up their minds to settle down as law-abiding agriculturists; but the authorities were mistaken. I don't know what happened to De Nam, but De Tham is still flourishing and is still carrying on the same game. The French have been fighting in Tonkin for the past twenty-seven years, and it looks as if they will have to go on fighting there for a good few years longer.

I myself saw no further fighting there, for a day or two after the evacuation of the fort I was struck down by the terrible blackwater fever, and that I am alive today is something approaching a miracle. I had felt out of sorts for some days, so much so that I have no clear recollection of the details of the final attack on the pirates' stronghold, and I had eaten practically nothing since my return from Phu-lang-Thuong; but I did not attach any importance to my; state, thinking that it was a simple attack of malaria, and that I should be doing the best thing possible by keeping on my feet and trying to shake it off. But I went to bed one night and lost all consciousness until I awoke in the hospital at Phulang-Thuong. This hospital was only a sort of field hospital, and hardly the place for such a serious case as mine was; but there was no choice, as to move me would have destroyed the small chance of life that I was held to possess.

Very few Europeans recover from the virulent fever which had attacked me, but I was so fortunate as to be an exception, and in a month's time I was sufficiently recovered to be moved to the big general hospital at Quang-Yen, which is near the sea, and in a very healthy situation in other respects. Here I was well looked after by the Sisters of Mercy, had a comfortable bed to lie in, and got all sorts of dainties to tempt my appetite. I had been there about a month and was quite convalescent when I unexpectedly received a shock by coming full tilt against Petrovski as I was walking in the grounds. I had enquired about him at Phu-lang-Thuong and had been told that he was dead; but here he was looking almost as well as ever, and, like myself, he had been made a sergeant. About a week after this we, with a good many others, were called before a medical board to be examined as to our fitness to return to duty; but the doctors evidently did not like the look of us, for they sentenced us both to be "repatriated," which in our case meant sending us back to Algeria.

Chapter 16

Volunteers for Dahomey

When we arrived at Oran on our return we were as well as we ever expected to be, and assumed that we would be sent direct to the depot to resume duty, but to our great surprise we were sent instead to the convalescent depot at Arseu, a little seaport town between Oran and Mostaganam. The convalescent depot was built on a range of high hills at the back of the town, in an ideal situation for the recovery of health, and as there was little or no restriction on our going and coming we put in three months here very pleasantly, loafing round the surrounding country and having a dip in the sea morning and evening.

Then we were sent back to Sidi-bel-Abbes, and, for the first time since our enlistment, were posted to different companies. I was detailed for duty in a camp that had been formed outside the town for the reception of recruits, and Petrovski remained in barracks, so we did not see as much of one another as was the case when we were last at the depot. Although I was under canvas I did not mind it, for it was not tent life under campaigning conditions, as we had beds and were pretty comfortable generally; but the monotony of the life soon began to oppress me again, and I was thinking of putting it to Petrovski that we would do well to volunteer again for Tonkin when the chance came round, when something even more stirring than service in the East offered itself.

My chum and myself were having dinner together in a cafe one night towards the end of July, when I picked up the *Echo d'Oran*, and read that a battalion of the Foreign Legion was to be formed for service in Dahomey under Colonel Dodds, of the Marine Infantry.

We made short work of the remainder of the dinner, and went into barracks to see if anything was known of it there, but although there was much excitement it was all based on the newspaper paragraph.

Next morning, at the reading of orders, however, the fact was officially announced, and volunteers were called for. Only four hundred men were wanted from our regiment—the other half of the battalion having to be found by the 2nd Etranger at Saida—but nearly every man in the depot volunteered. Then it was given out that preference would be given to seasoned men who had served in Tonkin, but this did not seem to increase our individual chances, as most of the sergeants were possessed of this qualification.

When we heard later, however, that the command of the battalion was to be given to Commandant Faraux we did think that we were well in the running, for we were both well acquainted with this officer, who had on more than one occasion complimented us. Things turned out as we hoped, and when the names of the selected were read out we had the satisfaction of finding ours among them.

The trouble between King Behanzin of Dahomey and the French had been brewing for some time, and things had now come to such a pass that the government of the Republic had decided to smash him utterly and have done with him. The king had been receiving some eight hundred pounds a year from the French as a sort of bribe for leaving the trading stations of Kotonou and Porto-Novo alone; and instead of wasting this money on musical boxes and so on, as would have been done by a less enlightened potentate, King Behanzin had used it to augment the fund he was getting together to buy Krupp cannon and Winchester rifles, for the purpose of making things hot for his paymasters when he felt himself strong enough. He had reached this state some time previously, and had latterly being annoying the French exceedingly.

On the morning of the 2nd August the Battalion of Dahomey marched out of the barrack gate, headed by the band of the regiment, and followed by the whole of the remainder of the regiment then in Sidi-bel-Abbes, with arms in their hands and the regimental colour flying in their midst. This was the second time I had left those barracks to go campaigning, and as the strains of the regimental march, "*Tiens voilà du boudin*" struck on my ear I thought of the lively lot that had marched with me behind that tune on the former occasion, and wondered if I should again be one of the lucky few to return undamaged, finally coming to the conclusion that the odds against me were much greater than when I set out for Tonkin.

As I was marching on the flank of the leading section I was much struck with the fantastic actions of the pioneer-corporal, who was, of course, marching at the head of the column. He pranced along as if he were practising for a two-step, and every now and then he would turn half-round and show a delighted grin which exposed a remarkably good set of enormous teeth. This corporal was a gigantic Alsatian, named Minnaert, and he had the reputation of being a somewhat eccentric fellow. At the taking of Son-Tay, in Tonkin, he was credited with being the first man to enter the enemy's fort and to have made an extempore tricolour out of the seat of his red trousers, a piece of his blue cummerbund, and a large white handkerchief, which flag he duly hoisted amid the laughter of the troops.

Only a day or two previous to the departure of the battalion for Dahomey he had greatly distinguished himself at a fire which had broken out in the house where Colonel Blanc, of the *spahis*, the officer commanding the garrison of Sidi-bel-Abbes, had lodgings; and a few days before that he had fallen upon a group of Spaniards who sneered at the Legion as he was passing them, and soundly thrashed the whole six.

When we arrived at the station the troops who were not going formed up in line facing the platform, as a sort of guard of honour, and the civil authorities, headed by the *sous-prefect*, came to pay us respect also.

We were soon in the special train, or rather the special carriages that were to be hooked on to the ordinary train from Tlemcen, and in three-quarters of an hour after we had left the barracks the train moved out of the station. It came to a stop when it had gone some fifty yards or so, and slowly moved back into the station again. Many of the superstitious legionaries looked upon this as a bad omen and openly expressed their regret at having volunteered for the job, and they were not comforted when it was discovered that the reason why the train had to return was because the enormous weight had broken one of the sleepers.

We got off eventually and arrived at Oran about midday. Here we found the band of the 2nd Zouaves waiting for us, and they played us to the artillery barracks, where a camp had been pitched for our accommodation. We had expected to embark the same day, but now found that the man-of-war that was to carry us had been detained at Toulon, and that we would have to wait at Oran for three or four days. There was great dissatisfaction at first, but this was turned into rejoicing when we found that the townspeople had made up their minds to fete us and make our stay pleasurable. The two companies from Saida joined us the same day, and partook of the festivities.

The inhabitants fell over one another in extending private hospitality to the legionaries, presents of tobacco, cigarettes, pocket-knives, and other little things were given lavishly, and we had a high old time all round. The officers were entertained publicly, and the non-commissioned officers were invited to a "punch," or big-drink function, at the Brasserie Soulier, at which half the town was present, and said kinder things of us than we had ever believed them capable of. It was a French rendering of Kipling's "*It's Tommy this, and Tommy that, and Tommy, get outside; but it's thank you, Mr. Atkins, when the trooper's on the tide.*" The French people love a legionary—when they want him.

On the 7th August the trooper came in, and the battalion was at once paraded. When the roll was called it was found that three men were absent, which, considering that a great many of the men were in the town when the "assembly" was sounded, was extremely satisfactory. These three men afterwards came running down to the wharf, as if they were afraid of being left behind, and in the meantime three *Zouaves* had shouldered the missing men's rifles and knapsacks and marched down with us, so their absence had caused no inconvenience. We were accompanied down to the wharf by an enthusiastic crowd, which had to be kept off us by a company of *Zouaves* when we formed up there preparatory to embarking.

We were just on the point of defiling on to the trooper when there was a clattering of hoofs and two mounted Chasseurs d'Afrique, followed by a general officer in uniform, burst through the crowd. This was General Metzinger, commanding the Oran sub-division. He had been a distinguished colonel of Zouaves and had served side by side with the legion, both in Algeria and Tonkin. After passing along the ranks, and stopping here and there to ask a man how many campaigns he had seen and what wounds he had received, he ordered us to close round in a semi-circle and addressed to us a few soldierly words to the effect that he was satisfied, from the look of us, that we were capable of doing anything that the Legion had yet done, and only wished that he was going with us to see us do it.

In another hour we were well out at sea. Our first stop was at Dakar, a French town situated on a kink in the African coast-line, about a mile south of Cape Verde. We arrived here on August 14th, and stayed two days to coal and take in fresh provisions. Dakar at that time was a new place, but three miles or so seawards is the island of Goree, which is an island with a history. It is a barren black basaltic rock, about three-quarters of a mile long and half-a-mile wide in the middle, from which it tapers to a point at each end. Small and barren as it is, some three thousand people live on it, and there is very little rock to be seen for buildings. It is strongly fortified, and used to be described as the key to West Africa, but from what I was able to see of the fortifications in the course of an afternoon's stroll round it, I am very doubtful as to its ever having deserved to rank as a West African Gibraltar.

As nothing grows on the island, all its supplies have to be brought from the mainland, and it is difficult to see how it could ever have been held in face of a hostile squadron. The interest of this island to an Englishman lies in the fact that it once belonged to us, and furnishes the only instance in our history of a colonial governor being hanged for an act done in his official capacity. In the early days of our West African colonies our ports there used to be garrisoned by a regiment called the Royal African Corps, which was recruited by drafting into it the hopelessly bad characters from the regular army. In 1782, when Wall was Governor of Goree, the paymaster of the troops wanted to slip away to England without settling up with the men, whose pay was much in arrears, and there was something like a mutiny.

Governor Wall was going to England with the paymaster, and was so much annoyed at the men's interference with his plans that he ordered three of the ringleaders, a sergeant and two privates, to receive 800 lashes each. The men died as a consequence of this punishment, and there was such an outcry in England when the facts became known that Governor Wall deemed it prudent to retire to the Continent. He stayed abroad for twenty years, and then, thinking that the affair had blown over, he returned to England and surrendered himself. It was a false move on his part, for he was at once brought to trial, convicted, and hanged at Newgate.

We were allowed to go ashore almost without restriction while the ship lay at Dakar, and Petrovski and I availed ourselves of the permission to the uttermost, visiting not only Dakar and Goree, but also Rufisque, on the other side of the inlet. In a *café* at Rufisque we met an extraordinary man. This man was a corporal in the Marine Infantry, named, if I remember rightly, Marthe. Some four years previously he had made free with a few *francs* of public money in his possession— the amount was less than a sovereign, I think he said—and deserted into the hinterland with no provision whatever for a journey, and no clear idea where he was making for. Here he was lucky enough to be picked up by a tribe of wandering Arabs, the Trarza.

He stayed with them for four years, becoming a sheik and travelling with them across the Sahara desert at its greatest width no less than four times, besides wandering into every nook and corner of the Soudan. Then he fell homesick and seized the opportunity of the tribe being in the desert to the north of Senegal to inform his hosts of his intention to visit his own people again. But the Arabs were too fond of him to let him go, and he had to make his escape by stealth and do a desert tramp "on his own." He managed, after many adventures, to reach an English trading post at Cape Juby, and there he was taken aboard an English ship and carried to Teneriffe, from whence he returned to Dakar and gave himself up to the military authorities.

A day or two before our arrival he had been tried by court-martial for desertion and embezzlement, with the result that he had been unanimously acquitted. Now, he told us, he was waiting for a ship to take him to France; but he did not intend to stay there, as he liked being a wandering Arab so much that he was going back to the Trarza after he had spent a little time at home with his friends. I never heard any more of him, and I have often wondered whether he did go back to the desert.

At mid-day on August 25th, seventeen days after leaving Oran, we cast anchor at Kotonou, in the *Bight of Benin,* and disembarked in the exciting and haphazard manner peculiar to the surf-bound West African coast.

Next day we were ordered to move on to Porto Novo, some fifteen miles distant. Porto Novo is the capital of the kingdom of Tofa, the king of which was very well disposed to the French. The monarch came and looked on quite affably while we were marched in, and didn't seem at all put out when we laughed at him. This was sensible of him, for I am afraid that he would have been laughed at just the same even if his feelings had been hurt. He had on a French naval officer's cap, and a richly embroidered frock coat, but nothing else whatever, and his general appearance was so comical that one was obliged to laugh.

CHAPTER 17

Death of Our Gallant Commandant

The day following our arrival at Porto Novo we were inspected by Colonel Dodds, who was nothing like what I had imagined him to be. I don't know whether the general had black blood in his veins, but he looked as if he had a lot. Ninety-nine people out of a hundred would have taken him for a *mulatto*, and it is quite possible that he may be one, as he was born at Saint Louis, in the French Senegal; but there is nothing of the half-caste in his manner of going to work. He looked us over in a way that told us that he was a soldier to his fingers' ends, and many were the expressions of satisfaction that we had got such a leader. Our satisfaction did not diminish, either, when we got to know him better.

At Porto Novo we were served out with light flannel campaign suits and large pith helmets, and it was not until eight days after our arrival that we were ready for a forward movement.

About two thousand men of the expeditionary force, of whom about eight hundred, belonging to the Marine Infantry and Marine Artillery, were Europeans, had been on the spot for some time, and a column had already marched forward by the left bank of the River Oueme.

On September 1st we of the Legion started to catch them up, but our progress was terribly slow, not averaging more than about four miles a day.

One hour we would be struggling through a mangrove swamp, and the next forcing our way through tall grasses that reached well above our heads and chopping our way through thick bush. We carried nothing except our arms and 150 rounds of ammunition per man, and even this light load was as much as we could struggle along with.

Every morning immediately after reveille each man, black or white, was obliged to take a long drink of quinine. After this we got the morning coffee and then set out and struggled on until ten, when we halted for the morning meal. Then on again until five, when we bivouacked for the night.

After eight days of this we joined the remainder of the force, and our battalion was split up among the three groups into which the expeditionary force was divided. Our battalion commander, Commandant Faraux, was placed in command of the second group, to which my company and another belonged, each of the other two groups having one company of the Legion.

On the 11th September, No. 2 Group advanced to Dogba, and on the 16th we made a strong reconnaissance along the left bank of the Oueme to Oboa without encountering a single human being.

On the following day the 1st Group established itself at Oboa, while we of the 2nd Group and the 3rd Group remained in camp at Dogba in a good defensive position, for which there seemed to be no need, as up to this time we had not seen the colour of the enemy, and our native scouts could give us no information regarding his whereabouts—that is, as far as could be ascertained by one occupying my humble position.

On the 18th we of the 2nd Group received orders to start before daylight next morning to open the road half-way to Oboa, so that the artillery could pass along it.

It was five o'clock on the morning of the 19th. Reveille had just sounded though it was still quite dark, and we of the 2nd Group were fumbling and groping around to get ready for our march when a shot rang out from an outlying picket, which was composed of Marine Infantry. We rushed to our arms and formed up, there were a few more shots, and then the picket came bounding into camp with thousands and thousands of black shadows close at the men's heels—the Dahomeyans had surprised us. As fast as we could ram the cartridges in and loose off we fired into the moving black shadows and saw them topple over like corn falling under the sickle. They checked momentarily and then moved sideways towards the staff tents.

"Now, legionaries, let us give 'em the bayonet," shouted Commandant Faraux.

"Ha! ha! now the Legion is going to hobnob with 'em and they'll enjoy themselves," laughed a corporal, who was standing close to me. "I wonder if these are the celebrated lady soldiers. If so, they'll find that it's dangerous to meet a legionary in the night time."

Before he had finished this remark we were on the run towards the threatened side of the camp, and in a few seconds more were in the thick of them, ramming our bayonets into their bodies until the hilt came up against the flesh with a sickening thud, and then throwing them off to make room for another, like a farm labourer forking hay, until we had to clamber over dead and dying men piled two or three high to get at the living.

For the moment there was no question of those of the enemy who were receiving our special attention running away. They couldn't run away, for the great mass behind was pushing them on to our bayonets. It was a terrible slaughter. And above the yells and curses of the combatant, above the shrieks and howls of the wounded, we heard the voice of Commandant Faraux shouting, "Come on, legionaries, come on."

After driving the bayonet charge well home we retired to re-form, and the enemy came on again. The legionaries then charged a second time, and, after a severe hand-to-hand tussle, again pushed them back.

Previous to the commencement of the fight many of the enemy's sharpshooters had been hoisted with ropes to the tops of the tall palm trees which fringed the open space on which the camp stood, and from these points had been pouring a plunging fire into us from the first moment of the attack, a sub-lieutenant of the Marine Infantry, the first man killed on our side, having been shot as he lay asleep in his tent before the alarm was given.

It was light when we charged for the second time, and the Dahomeyans in the treetops seemed now to be picking their marks instead of firing at random, and their special attention appeared to be directed to the officers. In general the enemy were wretched shots, which was in part explained by the fact that they rested the butt of the rifle on the thigh when firing, so that the bullets for the most part passed over our heads, but these men in the trees made good practice and must have been the crack shots of the Dahomeyan army. Commandant Faraux was quite close to me as we were moving on the enemy, and I suddenly heard him exclaim, as, for a moment, he stopped cheering us on: "*Je suis bien touché*" (I am well hit). That was his reception of what turned out to be a mortal wound. He continued to advance and encourage us notwithstanding; but presently he was hit again and fell to the ground. When the enemy had once more retired before the points of our bayonets, and we were again re-forming, the commandant was carried past us on his way to the ambulance. Then, without anybody giving the order, and while the enemy was pouring a heavy fire into us, every legionary spontaneously presented arms as the wounded officer was born by.

"I will give twenty-five *francs* for every one of those niggers you bring down out of those trees," said Colonel Dodds, who was standing near.

"We'll fetch 'em all down for nothing, colonel," replied a legionary grimly.

And fetch them down we did—later on. There was no time to attend to them just then, for the body of the enemy that was opposed to us had not yet had enough, and, led by a few Amazons, were coming on again. In the course of this rush a foolishly brave sergeant-major of Senegalese Spahis got right into the midst of the Amazons, who closed round him and took him away with them. Next day his body was found some distance away by a scouring party. It bore signs of the man having been tortured to death, and was mutilated in a manner which cannot be described.

By ten o'clock the Dahomeyan army was in full retreat, leaving behind about three hundred dead. To turn up the earth in order to bury this large number of corpses would have let loose sufficient fever germs to have infected the whole force, and to leave them on the ground to decompose would have been still more dangerous to health, so Colonel Dodds ordered them to be burned. As soon as the fight was over the native carriers were accordingly set to collect them into a vast funeral pyre which was started by a few tins of kerosene being poured over it, and burned with much unpleasantness for days. The collectors did not trouble to carry the enemy's dead—they simply put themselves between the legs of the corpses like a horse between the shafts of a cart and dragged them to the heap. Our own dead, in number about a dozen, were buried very deep, and their resting-place was hidden by being levelled and re-covered with turf to protect the remains from insult.

There were two little stern-wheel gunboats on the Oueme accompanying the expedition, and in the afternoon the severely wounded—among them two legionaries besides Commandant Faraux—were embarked on one of them for conveyance to Porto Novo.

Commandant Faraux was very popular with the legionaries, and all of us assembled to see him off, many of the men crying as he was carried past us with Colonel Dodds walking by the side of his stretcher, talking to him. He died at four o'clock next morning from the effects of the first of his two wounds, the bullet having lacerated the intestines and set up peritonitis. It was reported, I have no doubt truthfully, that his last words to Colonel Dodds before the gunboat left, were recommendations of certain men of the Legion who had behaved well in the fight.

This gallant officer was forty-three years of age when he was killed, and he had had a most interesting career. He enlisted in a line regiment as a private soldier in 1867 at the age of eighteen, and so greatly distinguished himself during the war with Germany that he was made captain in 1870, having then only three years' service, and being not yet twenty-one years of age. After the war, when the establishment of the army was reduced, he had either to retire or revert to the rank of lieutenant. He chose the latter, and did not reach the rank of captain again until 1876. Wherever there was service to be seen he was to be found, and after a brilliant career in Algeria and Tonkin he was appointed to the command of one of the battalions of the Legion serving in the East in 1889. He was one of those rare officers who seem to gain the real affection of their men without in any way becoming slack in matters of discipline, and when Colonel Dodds, in an order of the day, referred to his death as a catastrophe for France and for the Legion, he was saying no more than the bare truth.

We had taken a few prisoners, including two Amazons, all of whom were shot by way of reprisals for the torture and mutilation of the Spahi sergeant-major.

There was a lot of talk, at the time of this fight and afterwards, about the Dahomeyans having the assistance of Europeans. At one time it was reported that the chief military adviser of King Behanzin was an English deserter from Sierra Leone, but the rumours generally credited Germans with being the backbone of the Dahomeyan army. For my part, I do not think for one moment that the enemy had any skilled military assistance at all, inasmuch as the first thing any soldier would have put a stop to would have been the futile waste of ammunition involved in firing rifles from the thigh. At that time there was a tendency, however, to find Englishmen or Germans at the bottom of every colonial difficulty that the French met with, and it was assumed that any natives who made a stand against the French forces were assisted by trained English or German soldiers as far as I know without there being any foundation for such beliefs.

CHAPTER 18

Battle of G'bede

The day after the fight all hands were turned on to build a fort at Dogba. When completed this fort was named Fort Faraux, in memory of our late commandant. As soon as the fort was finished a small garrison was told off to it, and the main body of the expeditionary force moved forward towards the north along the bank of the river.

Owing to our having to make a practicable road for the artillery as we advanced we only got over the ground at the rate of two or three miles a day, and each night found us utterly exhausted.

On September 28th I made one of a party of the Legion which was embarked upon the gunboats *Opale* and *Corail*, for the purpose of pushing a reconnaissance in advance of the column to look for a ford which was reported to exist at a place a few miles upstream. We had reached the point where the ford was said to be, and were looking for it, when a heavy fire was opened on us from the right bank. There was nobody to be seen, for the Dahomeyans had ambushed themselves in tall grass behind a screen of trees; but we judged by the fire that they were present in some force, probably a thousand strong, and it was judged inexpedient to land our small detachment.

The bullets passed over our heads as usual, and our casualties were insignificant, but it was no part of the officers' plan to let the enemy stay there if they could be shifted with the force at command. It was decided, then, to tempt the Dahomeyans into the open, and with this end in view the gunboats steamed slowly up the stream until we came to a clearing, where the boats went close in to the shore as if they were disabled, and wanted to take the ground. The bait took, and the Dahomeyans poured into the clearing in hundreds and proceeded to attack us. When they were fully exposed we set about them with our Hotchkiss quick-firers and our rifles to such good effect that in a few moments there were heaps of dead on the plain, and the survivors were legging it away as fast as they could go.

This party of Dahomeyans were evidently posted there to prevent our crossing, and their opening fire on us and so disclosing their presence was a military error of which they would have hardly been guilty if they had had even a European lance-corporal to advise them. It was absolutely necessary that we should cross over to the right bank, and if they had played "possum" to the gunboats and ambuscaded the column as it was crossing the river, they could undoubtedly have caused us serious loss even if they could not prevent our getting over. As it was, the fire from the gunboats was so destructive to them that they decided not to wait for the main body and disappeared from the neighbourhood, not only leaving the ford uncovered but also deserting a fine bridge constructed of tree trunks, which seemed to have been recently built to enable the Dahomeyan army to cross over to our side. We discovered this bridge in the course of a further reconnaissance, and part of the column crossed over it instead of using the ford, the bridge being destroyed before we moved on.

After crossing to the right bank the column struck away from the river and soon came to two well-defined paths, or native roads, branching off from a fork. One of these was the direct road to Abomey, the capital, which we thought was the one we should take, but the colonel decided to take the other one, which led to Kana, the sacred fetish city of the Dahomeyans and the summer residence of the king.

On the 3rd October the colonel, hearing that the enemy had assembled in force on our front, set us to make a road through the bush for the artillery so that we could come upon the Dahomeyans in flank.

On the 4th October, at 5 o'clock in the morning, while it was still dark, we commenced the march which was to end in our coming to grips with the main body of the Dahomeyan army, which was estimated to be at least ten thousand strong. We marched without exchanging a word, and moving as silently as possible.

Towards nine o'clock our advance guard came into contact with an outlying body of the enemy, about a mile from the village of G'bede, and a few minutes afterwards the Dahomeyan battery of Krupp guns, said to have been obtained from German merchants at Whydah in exchange for cargoes of "free labourers" for the cocoa plantations, opened fire on us. Then the two squadrons of Senegalese Spahis, which were marching at the head of our column, were so furiously attacked by an overwhelmingly superior body of the enemy that they broke and retired on us in great disorder; but they at once re-formed and deployed in column of squadrons on the wings of the infantry.

Then a company of our Haussas, which followed the Spahis in the order of march, were taken in flank by a sudden discharge from the high grass and retired to the rear without stopping to make further enquiries.

The turn of the Senegalese Tirailleurs came next. A battalion of Amazons attacked them and gave them a very rough time indeed, but the *tirailleurs* stood their ground until reinforced by some Marine Infantry. Anyone inclined to sympathise with the Amazons on account of their sex, and look upon the combat between them and our men as unequal, may take it from me that their sympathy would be misplaced. These young women were far and away the best men in the Dahomeyan army, and woman to man were quite a match for any of us. They were armed with Spencer repeating carbines, and made much better use of them than the men made of their rifles; and for work at close quarters they had a small heavy-backed chopping sword or knife, very much like a South American machete, with which they did great execution.

They fought like unchained demons, and if driven into a corner did not disdain the use of their teeth and nails. One of them was seized and disarmed by a Marine Infantry man in this fight, but she was so far from being beaten that she at once turned on her captor and set about biting his nose off. The man yelled out for his mother, but the lady would not leave off worrying him until she was cut down by the sword of an officer who rushed to the man's assistance.

The uniform of these female warriors was a sort of kilted divided skirt of blue cotton stuff. This garment barely reached to the knees. It was supported at the waist by a leather belt which carried the cartridge pouches. The upper part of their bodies were quite nude, but the head was covered with a *coquettish* red *fez*, or *tarboosh*, into which was stuck an eagle's feather. These ladies were all exceedingly well developed, and some of them were very handsome, in a nigger kind of way.

Up to this time we of the legion had only been looking on, so we had a good opportunity of watching the charge of these furies, and we were much impressed and filled with admiration at their dash and gallantry. We learned to admire them more when we became opposed to them ourselves, which did not happen in this fight, however.

Our turn came when the fight had been in progress about half-an-hour. We were attacked by a body of the enemy some thousands strong, and we formed into company squares to resist their onslaught. As at Dogba our fire literally mowed down the advancing lines, but they came on again and again in the most determined manner, and there is no doubt in my mind that if they had been under capable European leadership we would have found ourselves in the very queerest of queer streets. As it was, they were compelled at last to retire to their entrenchments; but when we followed them and stormed the earthworks at the point of the bayonet they drove us back again and again.

When the fight had been in progress a couple of hours our two squadrons of Senegalese native cavalry charged the Dahomeyan artillery and sabred the gunners as they stood at their guns.

Then the whole strength of the infantry charged once more with the bayonet, and the blacks, led by Behanzin himself, set out as rapidly as they could for other parts. We pursued them to Poguessa, about two miles away, and were then recalled.

One incident of the pursuit that came under my notice was so remarkable that I hesitate to mention it, as it is pretty certain to be regarded as a mere traveller's tale.

A Dahomeyan warrior was killed while in the act of levelling his gun, from behind a cotton-tree, at Captain Battreau of the Legion, at point-blank range, and as he fell his rifle clattered down at the officer's feet. Captain Battreau, seeing that it was an old *Chassepot*, picked it up out of curiosity, and suddenly became very much interested in it. He examined it very carefully, and then exclaimed, with a gasp of astonishment:

"Well, this is something like a miracle! Here is the very rifle I used in 1870 during the war with Germany! See that hole in the butt? That was made by a Prussian bullet at Saint-Privat. I could tell the gun from among a million by that mark alone; but here's my number stamped on it as well, which is evidence enough for anybody. Who would have thought it possible that I could pick up in Africa, as a captain, a rifle that I used in France, as a sergeant, twenty-two years ago? It is incredible!"

The sceptical reader will probably think that the captain was "pulling our legs" a bit; but this explanation is inconsistent with the fact that the officer asked for and obtained special permission to keep the rifle as personal property on account of its associations, and he was hardly likely to have done this unless he could prove that it was, in fact, the identical rifle he had formerly used.

Our losses in the fight at G'bede were 5 Europeans—including two officers—and 4 Senegalese killed; and 20 Europeans—including 3 officers—and 13 Senegalese badly wounded.

The Dahomeyan dead were burned as before, and our own dead buried . Then we moved forward to the village of Poguessa, where we halted for the next day to rest and clean our arms.

CHAPTER 19

Fighting for Water

On the morning of the 6th several parties were sent out to feel for the enemy. The party I was with scoured the country until late in the afternoon without seeing any Dahomeyans except a dead one here and there—evidently wounded men from G'bede who had struggled on until they had dropped and died—and we were returning to camp when we heard the sound of heavy firing on our left flank. Our commander at once gave the order to change direction and march towards it.

"Give them the old tune, bugler, to let them know that the Legion is coming to hobnob with them," said the captain, and the stirring notes of the regimental march carried the promise of support to our comrades—who, as we learned afterwards, were very hardly pressed at that moment.

When we arrived on the scene we found that one of the other reconnoitring parties—consisting of three companies of Senegalese Tirailleurs—was disputing the possession of a bridge over a small stream with about five thousand Dahomeyans, and was palpably getting the worst of the deal. Forming into line, we fired volleys into the thick of them as we advanced, and then, when we got close, the order was given to fix bayonets and charge. Helter-skelter we went, and, after a short struggle at the bridge, drove the enemy before us right through a fortified camp which they had formed a short distance from the further bank of the stream in the apparent hope of barring our progress. When the Spahis charged the guns at G'bede they were unable to capture them, and the Dahomeyans had got them away and placed them in this fortified camp. If Behanzin's warriors had waited behind their entrenchments and peppered us with these guns as we came up we should have had a rough time of it, but, as it happened, they were of no service to them.

To account for the smart manner in which the Dahomeyans handled these Krupp field guns at G'bede it was said that they were manned by men who had belonged to the French Senegalese artillery, who had been recruited in Senegal by agents sent there by Behanzin for that purpose; but I cannot vouch for the truth of the assertion. There were so many wild rumours flying about the camp as to the composition of the king of Dahomey's army that I made up my mind to believe only what I saw; and I didn't see anything, beyond the un-doubted skill of the gunners, to lead me to attach any credit to this Senegalese artilleryman story.

Another yarn in circulation about this time was to the effect that the Spahis had captured four white men serving in Behanzin's army, and this report was so circumstantial that the men's names were given; but I saw no white prisoners, and never met anyone who did.

We were directed to hold the entrenched camp we had taken, and towards evening the rest of the force came up and occupied it. We had to stop here for four days, owing to heavy tropical rains, and it was not until the morning of the 10th that we resumed our march.

The line of march was then along the edge of a dense forest. There were an immense number of carriers with the column—mostly sub-jects of the king of Porto-Novo—about twice the number of com-batants—and most of them accompanied the expeditionary force very unwillingly, though they were well paid, and if they saw any chance they would throw down their loads and dive into the bush. The duty of shepherding them was entrusted to the Senegalese Spahis, and on this day I had an opportunity of seeing how they did it.

The colonel had sent me with a message to the commander of the rear-guard, and in passing along the length of the column I came upon an illustration of the treatment a black man in authority hands out to a brother black who happens to be bottom dog. A weak and feverish-looking carrier who was staggering along under his load sud-denly pitched forward on his face and lay on the ground as if unable to proceed further. Up to him rode a *spahi*, and, without any preliminary argument, commenced to belabour him with the flat of his sword. The carrier struggled to his feet and staggered a few paces towards the bush, in the evident intention of getting out of his tormentor's way, whereupon the *spahi*, without more ado, and as if he were doing the most natural thing in the world, coolly dug his sword into him a couple of times and settled him. Then he divided the dead man's load among three carriers who already had their full quantity, and got on his horse again as if he had just been performing an ordinary routine duty.

I went on my way, and when I came to a white sergeant of Spahis I reported the matter to him. He shrugged his shoulders and said his men had orders to kill any carrier trying to get away, and that I had better report the matter to his officer, who was behind, if I wanted to report it to anybody. I did report it when I came to the officer; but all I got from him was a half jocular remark to the effect that the Spahis were queer cattle, and that I had better leave them alone and set about picking the beams out of the eyes of my legionaries. Then I thought that I would have a go at Colonel Dodds himself when I reported to him after delivering my message, but before that time came I concluded that the matter had really nothing to do with me after all, so I said nothing.

We had made about ten miles when we came in sight of a village called Sabovi, and were halted while our artillery shelled it. When we eventually advanced we found the place deserted, and we cooked our evening meal on the fires that the Dahomeyans had lighted to cook theirs. We had suffered greatly from want of water on the march, and when we got to the village we could find no more than was sufficient for cooking purposes. Parties of us searched the neighbourhood for the source of the Dahomeyans' supply, but we could not find it, and we passed a very thirsty night in consequence.

It was here that I saw the barbarous punishment of the *crapaudine* applied for the only time it came under my notice. At one time this punishment ,used to be inflicted in barracks for even trifling offences, but General de Negrier put a stop to it, and a great many other abuses, when he was in command of the Algerian Army Corps, and it had fallen into such disuse that I had never seen it up till then. On this night at Sabovi during the search for water an Italian who belonged to the Legion got at loggerheads with a sergeant and struck him. When they returned to camp the sergeant reported the occurrence, and it was decided to punish the man with the *crapaudine*. It must be remembered that in most armies he would have been tried by drum-head court-martial and shot.

He was stripped naked, his hands were pinioned behind his back, and his ankles were tied together. Then his ankles were lashed to his wrists, and he was thrown on the ground looking very much like a trussed fowl. The agony incidental to this constrained position must have been almost beyond human endurance after a time; but in this poor man's case the punishment was intensified by the fact that in no long time after he was tied up his body was literally covered with a swarm of black ants—and anyone who has been in tropical Africa will know what that means. After the man had been in this position about an hour his cries were agonising. To stop them a gag was placed in his mouth, which had the effect of reducing his cries to much more distressing moans. The man was eventually released after about three hours of it, and he was then so ill that he had to be taken to the hospital, and did no more duty during the campaign.

I have a very strong opinion that in almost every case of a private soldier striking a superior the superior is in some way to blame; and in this particular case there was only too much reason to suppose that the row was brought about by a tactless sergeant unnecessarily irritating a man whose nerves were on the stretch. Every man who is placed in authority over other men ought to have it impressed upon his mind that treacle is a better medium for catching flies than vinegar.

On the 11th we did not move. This was rather a good thing for us as in the afternoon the rain came down in torrents, and by spreading out the tent-flaps we were able to catch enough to drink our fill, which was a great treat, and to replenish our water-bottles with more palatable stuff than the muddy and poisonous swamp water we had been drinking lately.

We resumed our onward march at five o'clock on the morning of the 12th. Between seven and eight o'clock, after we had gone about four miles and had traversed the deserted village of Ouabomedi, we were toiling painfully through thick bush when a heavy fire was poured into us from above. We had to return the fire at random, for we could not see the enemy, and this unsatisfactory sort of fighting continued for some time before we were ordered to force our way through the bush and charge the Dahomeyan position at the point of the bayonet. When we had struggled through the bush we found that our adversaries were firing from three trenches, one behind the other, on the slope of a small hill, and it seemed to be a somewhat difficult proposition to dislodge them.

We charged these trenches several times from the front and were repulsed. Then we went round and turned the position, which we captured after three hours' fighting. The Legion had three killed in this affair. We buried them on the spot and then sat down and enjoyed, as best we could, a morning meal without a drop of anything to drink, although the heat was stifling and we were parched with the exertions of the fight. We took a few prisoners, who told us with every appearance of satisfaction that a warm time was awaiting us in front, and that few of us would live to make the return journey.

At two o'clock in the afternoon, still thirsty, we resumed our march, following what appeared to be a regularly used track. Hardly had 'we got on the road than we were attacked again, both from the front and the flank, and had another couple of hours' fighting before the enemy was beaten off. Four killed and twenty wounded was the total of our bill for this.

When we reached the place where it was decided to camp for the night everyone was so utterly exhausted that we pitched ourselves on the ground and went to sleep in the open, without troubling to eat or to pitch our tents. We wished we hadn't been so lazy before the night was over, for the rain came down in torrents and we were wetted to the skin. There were compensations, however, for the same rain that drenched us provided us with satisfaction for our devouring thirst.

Next morning we learned that some of our spies had come in during the night with the intelligence that we were surrounded, and that in our front was an entirely new Dahomeyan army entrenched behind the River Koto, whose banks, being steep and rocky, could be easily held against us. Five o'clock in the morning found us once more on the march forward, however, and six o'clock found us once more in action. The brunt of this fight fell on my company, which formed the advance guard of the force, and had four men killed and fifteen wounded. We were fired at from an ambush in the long grass, and did not see a single Dahomeyan until we compelled them to show themselves by charging with the bayonet into the vegetation that hid them. Then we got them on the run and followed them to their camp, which we took possession of.

We had buried our dead and were standing about, with our rifles in the crooks of our arms, eating a dry meal of biscuit and tinned meat, when the Dahomeyans sneaked up again and sent a shower of bullets into us, which killed one legionary and wounded another. We fired a volley or two in the direction the shots came from, and then sallied out after the shooters with the bayonet, but they didn't wait for us and left us in peace for the remainder of the day and night. We lay down that night very thirsty indeed—during the whole of that long, hot, tiring day we had not a single drop of water.

Next day we fared even worse, for there was no water for the

131

morning coffee and we had to start on the march with black cracked lips and swollen tongues. In the course of the day we came across some small pools of water, so muddy and disagreeable that the thirsty horses would not touch it. We thirsty men actually fought for it, and those who were fortunate enough to get some thought it delicious.

Towards noon we came in sight of a forest which seemed to be situated in a hollow. The greenness of the vegetation suggested that there was water there, so we made our way toward it with hopeful feelings. On entering the wood the impression that we were near water was strengthened by our being beset by swarms of big vicious mosquitoes which drew blood from our hands and faces at every bite. We were not deceived. We found a sandy hollow with a large spring of beautifully clear water bubbling from its centre. But the enemy was in hiding round the edge of the clearing and peppered us all the time we were filling our camp-kettles and water-bottles.

We took no notice of them, however, for our business was the getting of water, and went on filling every receptacle belonging to the force. Down went our captain and three of our men, but we did not budge until we had filled everything that would hold water, and then we made our way out again without seeing a single Dahomeyan, though they were firing at us, almost at point-blank range, all the time. That night we encamped on an elevated plateau, which put us somewhat out of reach of the bullets of the enemy, who hovered round us and sniped us all night.

CHAPTER 20

Some Water at Last

We were now near the Koto River, and next morning it was decided to send parties down to get water from it. This was a much more difficult operation than it was at first supposed to be, for the banks of the river just there were covered by an impenetrable tropical jungle through which there were only a few narrow paths. Our watering party, made up of carriers bearing camp-kettles with one soldier from each section to direct them, was preceded down one of these paths by a company of Haussas. They had no sooner got well into the thicket than the enemy opened fire on them. The volume of the firing told us in the camp that there was going to be more trouble in getting the water than had been anticipated. Then the terrified native carriers, who had thrown down the camp-kettles and bolted at the first shot, came straggling in and the order was given to the buglers to sound "Retire at the double" to bring in the escort.

When our men did not appear in response to this call it was realised that their retreat was cut off and two sections of my company were ordered to go to their assistance. With bayonets fixed and brought down to the "charge" we started off at the "double," and in the course of a few minutes found ourselves in a regular inferno, being under the fire of thousands of the enemy whom we could not see. Our men fired volleys into the bush on either side of us as we pushed our way onwards, but the Dahomeyans had us at a great disadvantage as we could not get at them with the bayonet, and were compelled to fire at random, while they could see us. When we at last came in sight of our hard-pressed comrades we found them beset by a large body of the enemy, whom we had to charge with the bayonet three times before they would give way. Then the order was given to retreat, and back we went, without a drop of the much-desired water, picking up our dead and wounded as we receded under the terrible hail of bullets.

An old legionary of twenty-four years' service—one of the survivors of the bloody fight outside Orleans in 1870, in which two battalions of the Legion were practically wiped out—was grumblingly criticising our officer for ordering us to retreat instead of forcing our way to the water, saying that he would rather be shot than be thirsty, when he suddenly stopped and fell to the ground badly wounded, remarking with a curse that he was now both shot and thirsty.

Then the officer went down, and, after him, the sergeant-major. As I was now the senior of those now on their feet I moved up to take command of the detachment, when the officer got up again with his left arm dangling uselessly at his side, and with a cheery, "All right, sergeant, I'm not outed yet," resumed the direction of the retreat.

The Dahomeyans followed us into the open and surrounded us in such numbers that things looked desperate indeed. It would, I am afraid, have been impossible for us to have got back to camp unaided; but our predicament had been seen and the whole battalion of the Legion was sent to our support at the "double." The Dahomeyans replied to this by bringing up more troops, and it was soon necessary to bring the whole of the expeditionary force into action. With all our strength, however, we could not dislodge the enemy from the thick bush, and could not, consequently, get at the water. Many Amazons were with the Dahomeyans in this fight and seemed to hold positions of authority, for there were some with every body of men, leading them on and encouraging them.

Possibly they were inciting the male warriors to show themselves worthy of having an Amazon for a wife, which was, at that time, the highest form of military reward in Dahomey. One Amazon, in particular, was very enterprising. She deliberately advanced to within a couple of dozen paces of the officer commanding the battalion of the Legion and put a bullet into his chest. This made the legionaries angry, and I am afraid that few of the Amazons employed against us that day got away with a whole skin. The bravery and the military skill of these women soldiers filled us all with admiration, and we were pretty well agreed that if the whole of the Dahomeyan army had been made up of them it would have taken a much larger force than ours to have got to Abomey.

The only officer killed on this day was, strangely enough, not in the firing line at all. He was a brother of the sergeant-major whom I have previously mentioned as having been eaten by a tiger in Tonkin, and a bullet found him while he was engaged on some duty right in the centre of our camp.

There were half-a-dozen officers badly wounded, however, one of whom afterwards died, and none of them did any further duty with the expedition. Of men killed in the fighting of the past three days there were 17, and 79 wounded.

The percentage of officers killed and wounded in this expedition was very high, about one in three, which was more than three times the percentage of casualties in action among the non-commissioned officers and men. The Dahomeyans seemed to pick out the officers, which was easy enough at point-blank range, and the officers helped them to do it by going into action wearing their decorations.

The misery of the wounded for want of a drop of water to moisten their parched lips was painful to witness, but we had no water to give them.

Colonel Dodds must have been of opinion that we were on the edge of a disaster, for as soon as it got dark that night we got the order to strike camp; and, carrying our dead with us, we retired to the camp we had occupied four nights before—on a plateau overlooking the deserted village of Apka.

In spite of our exhaustion and the difficulty of marching in the dark we arrived at our destination before midnight. The Spahis who, being mounted, were much fresher than the infantry, went out to find some wells which our chief had heard of as being in the neighbour-hood and not occupied by the enemy, while the remainder of the column, too done up to pitch tents, simply dropped to the ground. I fell asleep almost immediately, in spite of the torture I was suffering from thirst, and the rest-disturbing attentions of an army of black ants and myriads of mosquitoes, and did not awake until I was aroused, at about three o'clock, by Petrovski with the glad announcement that the Senegalese Spahis had arrived with water—enough for a present long drink round and the morning coffee.

We waited patiently enough until the sick and wounded had been supplied; but after this had been done there was not much regard paid to discipline or rank, and anyone who wanted water had to scramble for it.

Then, before daylight, a severe storm burst over us, the camp was flooded, and we had a great deal more water about us than we had any use for.

We learned on the morning of the 16th that Colonel Dodds had sent down to the coast for every available man to be sent up, together with further supplies, and that we were to stay where we were until they arrived. We were only about ten miles distant from Abomey, our objective, with the holy city, Kana, between us and the capital, but even if we had not had to wait for reinforcements I think that we should have had to halt for a few days to recuperate. A goodly number of the Europeans, probably twenty *per cent,* who were still doing duty were suffering from dysentery in a mild form, which would probably become severe enough to incapacitate most of them if we had another week like the last, and the native carriers were entirely demoralised, and needed to pull themselves together, while even those of us who enjoyed good health felt the need of a spell of rest.

The rest we got, though, was only comparative, for on the 16th we had a full day's work putting the camp in a state of defence, and for the next three days we had to put in all the time when we were not on duty in the entrenchments in trying to improve—the dilapidated condition of our clothing and boots. Day and night we were enveloped in a cloud of mosquitoes, which fought valiantly for the enemy as our faces and hands testified, while the merry little jigger made his presence felt in the feet of very many of us, and had to be dislodged by being picked out, like a winkle from its shell, with the point of a needle.

Although the enemy were in force at the fortified position of Kotopa, about two miles in our front, and we could see them quite plainly, they let us alone and we didn't trouble them until the 20th, when our moving our camp back about five hundred yards, so that we could straddle the road by which the reinforcements must arrive, brought on a conflict. We commenced the movement about midday, and had arrived at our new position, and, piling our arms, were engaged in digging earthworks to protect us, when we were assailed by a heavy fire. We took no notice of this for a time, but went on digging. Soon, however, we were compelled to take up our arms and form a defensive square, for we became surrounded by about three or four thousand of the enemy, who seemed bent on giving us a warm time.

Before we had commenced to move the camp our water-fatigue had gone out to the wells, which were about a couple of miles from our camp, and these men, most of them unarmed, were now cut off. We hardly expected to see any of them attempt to break through the enemy to get to us, and we were therefore surprised, and it must be confessed somewhat amused, to see an unarmed legionary sprinting towards us with a gigantic Dahomeyan close at his heels. The nigger was armed with one of the heavy-backed short swords, which I have previously described as being very much like a Cuban machete, and every now and again he would race up close to the legionary and make a cut at his head.

But every time he did this the legionary must have heard his approach, for no sooner was the machete raised in the air than our comrade would put on a desperate spurt and draw away again. It was a real sporting sprint-race, with a man's life for the prize, and it was so interesting that both we and the enemy temporarily stopped firing to watch it. The legionary won by a short head, so to say, the gallant black pursuing him right up to the muzzles of our rifles and meeting his death at the hands of a Senegalese Tirailleur who was devoid of the sporting instinct.

For three hours or more the enemy pressed us hard, so much so that it was we and not they who were giving ground, when we suddenly heard firing in their rear, and shortly afterwards they broke and retreated in disorder. This diversion in our favour was made by a party that had gone out in the early morning on a reconnaissance in force, and had returned just in time to take the Dahomeyans in rear at a critical moment.

During this action the Dahomeyans used against us an old French *mitrailleuse*. It made a strange crackling noise, the like of which I had never heard before, but it was recognised with some hilarity by an old adjutant of the Legion, who said that it would amuse them and not do us much harm. As a matter of fact I do not think that a single man was wounded by a *mitrailleuse* bullet, though I think that was more the fault of the gunners than of the gun, for showers of bullets from the machine whizzed over our heads. It was just the reverse with the enemy's artillery, however. They made capital practice on us from their entrenched camp at Kotopa, many of their shells pitching right into our midst, but owing to the badness of the fuzes the shells wouldn't burst.

Much to our surprise, all the members of the water-fatigue party except two found their way into camp, having dispersed and hidden themselves in the long grass until the coast was clear for their return. One of them, a bugler, was nearly walked over by a retreating party of the enemy; but he cleverly and with much presence of mind saved himself by sounding the "charge," and thus making the Dahomeyans believe that they had fallen into an ambush, with the result that they started off away from him at the run. The bodies of the two missing men were not found, nor was anything ever heard of them.

The fight was over about half-an-hour when we heard the joyous sound of the regimental march of the Legion in the distance, to the east of us. It turned out that it proceeded from the first part of the reinforcements, escorting a convoy of provisions.

Next day the Dahomeyans came on again in force, but they were driven off somewhat easily this time.

On October 24th the remainder of the reinforcements joined us, and on the following day, being now stronger by 600 men and with a good supply of provisions, we struck our camp at Akpa and resumed the offensive.

We got down to the river bank, opposite to where we had been encamped, without being opposed, and two of the three divisions of the force crossed over and established themselves on the heights on the other side. Two envoys from King Behanzin now turned up, preceded by two large white flags borne by two gigantic Dahomeyans; but Colonel Dodds apparently would have nothing to say to them, for they were presently seen making their way out of our lines in a very dejected condition.

Half-an-hour after the departure of the envoys we were charging the enemy's advance post at the point of the bayonet. The Dahomeyans did not make much of a stand here, and we had only half-a-dozen men wounded. These we left behind us, with the baggage, under the protection of two companies of Senegalese and two guns, and moved forward, after a quarter-of-an hour's breather in the captured post.

We had hardly turned our backs on the post when the sound of firing behind us told us that the enemy had returned and attacked the Senegalese, but we did not turn back to their assistance, our commander doubtless thinking that they would be able to hold their own, which proved to be the case.

Contrary to general expectation, we got no further fighting on this day, for our progress was hindered by a violent storm, which wetted us all to the marrow of our bones, but, as a compensation, gave us plenty to drink. Wet through as we were, and without any baggage, which we had left behind, we bivouacked on the sodden ground and passed a most miserable, sleepless night, the enemy sniping us fitfully.

We were on the move long before the break of day, and at dawn were before the Dahomeyans' second line of defence. The artillery opened the ball against the two rows of entrenchments which comprised this second line, and when the guns had prepared the way a little we advanced, as usual, with fixed bayonets, under a hellish fire. This was the toughest bit of fighting we had yet come across. The Dahomeyans fought desperately and would not give way. We charged right up to their earthworks time after time, but had to retire and re-form again and again without being able to get close enough to them to make an effective use of the bayonet. It was only after a very hard day's fighting that we possessed ourselves of the earthworks and bivouacked on the ground.

Next day we carried the attack forward to the two large forts of Kotopa, where Behanzin had concentrated the main force of his second line. These two forts were expected to prove a stiff job, for they were palisaded and defended by five Krupp guns and several *mitrailleuses*, according to the information collected by our intelligence department. The guns, however, were early dismounted and put out of action by our artillery, though the Dahomeyans managed to take them away when they retreated, and the troops of King Behanzin must have been somewhat discouraged by the results of the two previous days' encounters with us, for there was no repetition of the severe struggle of the day before, as, when once we got among them, they offered so little resistance that the attack became a mere butchery. Our losses in this three days' fight were only ten killed and seventy-three wounded, against an estimated loss to the Dahomeyans of two thousand five hundred.

Next morning, before daylight, the Dahomeyan army nearly brought off a disastrous surprise. We were attacked by an army estimated to number 15,000 men—and women—and before we realised that we were attacked at all quite a thousand of them were right in the midst of us. This was a very narrow squeak indeed, and the fight lasted the whole of the day, only ceasing when we had chased the Dahomeyans to within a mile of the walls of Kana.

In this pursuit I came across an instance of the extraordinary penetrative power of the *Lebel* rifle bullet. On coming up to a large cotton tree I saw three Dahomeyan corpses lying behind it, and noticing that one wore the distinctive dress of the Amazons I went to examine her closely. From the position of the bodies it was evident that the two men and the woman had been standing in line behind the tree, and that they had all fallen at the same time. This struck me as being very curious, the more so as they were well covered by the tree, and I looked closely to see how they had been killed.

139

Then I came to the conclusion that they must have been killed by the same bullet, and a hole right through the tree-trunk showed that this bullet had passed through about three feet of wood before it got to them. To look at wounds caused by the *Lebel* bullet one would think that they had been inflicted by ammunition not authorised by the rules of civilised warfare, so ghastly were they.

This dead Amazon was a very handsome and beautifully proportioned young woman, and her dead face bore a particularly mild and peaceful expression, utterly at variance with the bloodthirsty-looking machete in her girdle and the Winchester repeating carbine lying by her side. She had a very massive ring, made of particularly brassy-looking West African gold, on the second finger of her left hand. Not having any sentimental scruples about robbing a dead enemy, I took possession of this ring. It was a particularly fine example of what is known on the West Coast of Africa as a "Zodiac" ring, so-called because they have the signs of the zodiac engraved round them. On this one the signs of the zodiac stood out in heavy relief, as did also the rim of the ring. The signs and the rim were very solid-looking, and were brightly burnished, while the background of the signs was rough and dull. It was altogether such a well-made and effective ornament that I could not believe that it was of native manufacture. This kind of ring is common all down the West Coast, from Goree to the Cameroons, and it would be very interesting to know the origin of it.

I wore that particular ring as a scarf-ring for some time. It disappeared during a stay at Sierra Leone—I imagine that it provided too great a temptation to my house-boy, who was honest enough not to touch money that was left lying about.

CHAPTER 21

Capture of Muako

On the 20th November, much refreshed by the rest, we resumed our march, and on the same day attacked the fort of Muako, a strong position to the east of Kana. Our artillery battered the walls well, but, notwithstanding this, it took us all that day and the next to get a footing in the fort, and when we had driven the enemy out and sent them flying o'er the face of the country, they were rallied by a body of Amazons, who led them in a desperate but unsuccessful attempt to retake the fort.

On the 4th we moved on Dioxoue, a sort of suburb at a little distance from Kana, and here the Dahomeyans made the most determined stand of the campaign. In this fight the enemy was not opposed to us in such overwhelming numbers as they had been on most of the previous occasions of our meeting, but there were a great many more Amazons than we had as yet seen in a single fight, and they not only fought like furies themselves, but made the men, by their taunts and their example, fight better than we had ever seen them do. For some hours, so far from its being a case of driving the Dahomeyans out, they were the attackers, and we were compelled to form defensive squares to hold our own.

There were no less than six such squares at one period of the fight, and every one of them was as busy as the biggest glutton for fighting could desire. The Dahomeyan artillery was annoying us very much, and the Spahis were sent to charge the guns and stop it. They executed this order with great gallantry, taking four Krupps and several prisoners. It was rumoured in the camp that among these prisoners were an Englishman and a German, but I saw no white prisoners and do not believe that there were any.

We had been fighting since five in the morning under a broiling sun, and we were faint for want of food and water. It was now two in the afternoon, and the Dahomeyans, notwithstanding the loss of their guns, seemed to be a long way off being beaten. Suddenly, for no reason that we could see, the enemy started to run away as if they were executing some military movement by word of command.

As a matter of fact they were running away by order, for King Behanzin, who commanded in person, had had enough of it, and probably did not think it dignified to run away himself and leave his troops still fighting—he wanted company in his flight. This withdrawal of his troops, while there was still plenty of fight left in them, goes to show that Behanzin was anything but a first-class fighting-man himself, and that he personally deserved the rude remarks of the Amazons much more than the men to whom they were addressed.

The king and the troops with him didn't retire into Kana, but moved off along the Abomey road, leaving the garrison of Kana to do the best it could. We had fourteen killed and about fifty wounded in the taking of Dioxoue—a remarkably small casualty list considering the severity of the fighting.

In this fight there was an incident that was duplicated years afterwards by Piper Findlater at Dargai. It will be remembered that the piper received the Victoria Cross for continuing to play his pipes sitting down, after having been shot through the ankles. Well, that was history repeating an almost exactly similar incident that happened at Dioxoue. A bugler of the Legion was blowing the regimental march when he was hit in the legs. He sat down and coolly continued to blow until he fainted from loss of blood. So far as I am aware he got no reward. As a matter of fact, for every gallant deed that gets recognition, in every army, there must be at least a dozen that go unrewarded because they were not witnessed by anyone who had position and inclination to bring them to notice the men who are awarded Victoria Crosses, and such-like rewards, however much they may have deserved them, are very lucky to get them.

That night we bivouacked so near to the walls of Kana that the Dahomeyan artillerymen in the town pitched many shells right into the middle of our camp, and our casualties would have been heavy if the ammunition had been as good as the shooting. Luckily for us, the fuzes would not act, and none of the shells burst.

Kana stood on high ground, and the houses, which were mostly built of sun-baked bricks made of red ferruginous earth, were in clumps—like separate villages within an encircling wall. This town

142

wall was high and thick. It was built of the same sort of materials as the houses, and there were half-a-dozen substantial and formidable-looking bastions distributed round its circumferance. Altogether, the place looked as if it was going to give us a considerable amount of trouble.

After morning soup our artillery started shelling the town, and kept it up until a breach had been made, which was at about three o'clock in the afternoon. We now got the order to advance to the assault. As a considerable part of the town showed above the walls, we had for some time previous to this seen the Dahomeyans running about in a distracted manner as if they were in a terrible funk; so we did not expect to meet with a very determined resistance. No doubt the garrison had been demoralised by the desertion of the king. If Behanzin had stood his ground here it is very probable that we should have found Kana too tough a nut for our small force to crack, and the king might have been able to obtain terms of peace that would have left him the throne, at least. As it was, the Dahomey an army and the inhabitants practically departed from one side of the town as we were entering at the other, and we met with very little resistance indeed.

On entering we pushed our way to an inner wall that seemed to enclose about a fourth of the whole space enclosed by the outer wall. The gates of this enclosure stood open, and there was nobody to oppose our progress. Inside there was a collection of buildings much larger than any others in the town. As we approached the nearest of these a big negro came out and was promptly seized. He protested in shockingly bad French, saying that he was a headman of our own carriers, backing up this assertion by producing documentary proof of it. Being asked what he was doing there, he said with a grin that he had entered the town with us, but knew his way about it as he had been there before, and that he was just looking round to see if he could happen across a drop of rum or gin—he was sure there was plenty in the place if one could find it.

Our captain reminded him that the carriers were strictly forbidden to loot, and that if he was found doing it he would most assuredly be shot; whereupon the nigger, still grinning, remarked that the French were "dam-nonsense" men to work for. He said this in English and it was, perhaps, just as well for him that the officer did not understand it. I softened it in translating to a denial of knowledge of any order against drinking any liquor that could be found, and this explanation satisfied the captain, who ordered the man to show us round the place if he knew it.

The headman replied to the effect that he knew the place very well, as he had been in Kana many times. He went on to explain that we were now in the royal palace, and the headquarters of the Dahomeyan religion.

His talk was a curious mixture of Coast French, Coast English, and, now and again, an excursion into what was presumably his own language; but for all this he proved to be very useful as a guide and we got a lot of information from him. I learned from him that he was originally a subject of the King of Tofa, but that he had worked in English and French trading houses for many years, and that he had actually taken part in carrying up some of the very arms with which the Dahomeyans were fighting us.

The first building he took us into he called the "House of Sacrifice." At first sight this place appeared to be paved with very large whitish cobble-stones, but on our guide touching his head suggestively, with a grin, and then pointing to the floor, we examined it closer and found that the "cobble-stones" were really the tops of human skulls that had been rammed down into the earth to make a flooring. In the centre there was an enormous stone basin with a dried reddish sediment at the bottom of it, and dark red and black smears down the sides. The place stank like you might imagine a slaughter-house to stink if it had been used continuously and never cleansed from one year's end to another; and big loathsome flies were there in myriads. It was, in fact, the slaughter-house for the human cattle who were killed by the hundred on every occasion of national sorrow or national joy.

The chief of these functions was called the "Grand Custom." Our guide claimed to have been present at the "Grand Custom" which signalised the death of Behanzin's father, who was supposed to have been poisoned by his impatient son, and the accession of Behanzin himself.

At daybreak on this occasion, he said, a hundred men and a hundred women were put to death in order to start the day well. Then the new king emerged from his palace and about two hundred officers and princes saluted him and offered him their humble contributions towards the day's proceedings, namely: Four slaves each for slaughter, say, eight hundred human beings in all, sheep, goats, money, and rum. The king then proceeded to the royal sepulchre and superintended the burial in it of sixty living men, fifty living sheep, fifty living goats, forty living cocks, and a great quantity of *cowries*—native shell money.

This done, the king took a walk round the outside of the palace. When he arrived at the principal entrance he found there fifty men to do him honour by being killed in his presence.

After this the king mounted a platform and addressed a jingo speech to his subjects, afterwards rewarding them for listening to him by gifts of cowries, clothing and rum. Following this there was a sort of "go as you please" competition in murder among the spectators. Twenty-four living men were brought out, the body of each one being enclosed in a wicker basket, the head being left exposed. This wicker basket arrangement was probably invented to prevent the man inside objecting to the proceedings in such a way as to spoil sport. The baskets were stood up in a row facing the king, whilst the eager crowd of his loyal subjects stood behind, waiting for the word "Go." When the king made the sign to start the crowd made a break for the unfortunate twenty-four in the baskets, and a strenuous scrimmage took place round each one. The persons who emerged from these scrimmages bearing the head of one of the men in the baskets were winners of a string of *cowries*, the exchange value of which was about two shillings.

Among other parts of the palace enclosure pointed out to us, perhaps the most interesting were the tombs of previous kings of Dahomey. All of them were said to have been built of bricks made without water—the earth was wetted with human blood instead.

CHAPTER 22

Triumphal Return to Sidi-bel-Abbes

One of the four roads leading from Kana was a particularly fine grassy avenue, quite thirty yards wide, and bordered by grand old trees. We regarded this road with satisfaction, for it was the road to Abomey and promised us easy marching for the last stage of our journey. It was expected that we would move on at once, but for some reason which I did not learn, though there were many rumours, we were kept under the walls of Kana until the 16th November. During this prolonged halt Colonel Dodds made a very complimentary speech to us legionaries, telling us, among other things, that he considered us to be the finest soldiers in the world, and that he was extremely proud of having had the privilege of commanding us. It was no news to us that we were the finest soldiers in the world—we had all known that since our first week in the corps—but we liked being told so, and we swallowed this incontrovertible fact just as greedily as if it had been the rankest flattery.

The day before we moved forward to Abomey we learned that Colonel Dodds had got his "stars"—in other words, that he had been promoted to the substantive rank of General of Brigade—and the whole force spontaneously filed past his tent and respectfully saluted him. A number of other promotions were made known at the same time, among them being several of the Legion officers, two of our captains being promoted into line regiments as *commandants*—in the French army rewards follow very quickly upon the services which are held to have deserved them.

After setting fire to Kana we started on the march to Abomey at five o'clock in the morning on the 16th November. When we had gone about seven miles upon the beautiful broad turfy avenue that was called the Abomey Road, we found ourselves on an eminence that overlooked the capital at a distance of about a mile. We halted there. In the afternoon an envoy from Behanzin, with a white flag, came into camp. It was said that he had come with a message from the king in answer to one which our general had sent the day before, to the effect that he had burned Kana and was coming to perform the same operation on Abomey. The rumour now was that the envoy had brought a message from King Behanzin to the effect that he would save General Dodds the trouble of burning Abomey—he would do it himself.

Immediately after the departure of the envoy the order was given for us to get a move on, the general's idea no doubt being to prevent the escape of the king. Even as we were forming up we saw thin curls of smoke rising from several quarters of the town, which told us that Behanzin had lost no time in carrying out his threat.

In less than an hour we had completely invested the three sides of the town, but before we could close our circle the Dahomeyan army and such of the inhabitants of the capital who had not already left were able to get away, and as it was now getting dark we were unable to follow them.

The town was now well ablaze, and there was nothing to do but to let it burn itself out. Next morning, November 17th, the town was nothing but a smoking ruin, but some of the outside fortifications seemed to be uninjured . We marched on these but found them de-serted, and we entered the capital of Dahomey without firing a single shot or seeing a living Dahomeyan.

Abomey stood on a great deal of ground. It was, in fact, a real garden city, for almost every house was surrounded by a large garden, generally with trees in it. The walls of the houses were built of little stones embedded in the red earth of the country, and the fire had not done them much harm, but the roofs were made of thatch and had, of course, been utterly consumed. Before leaving, the inhabitants had destroyed everything in the way of furniture or utensils, but in many of the houses there were bottles of trade gin, said to be distilled in Germany from sawdust, and demijohns of trade rum, which is the same spirit as the gin but differently flavoured.

I even found a bottle of whiskey. There was a label on the bottle depicting a Highlander in the Stuart tartan dancing a sword dance, but the liquor inside belonged to the same family as the rum and gin. Poisonous as the stuff was, its discovery was hailed with delight by the troops, but their joy didn't last long, for as soon as the general heard of the find he ordered all the stuff to be given up and destroyed, and this happened before the finders had found opportunity to drink more than a tot or two of it. We were not allowed to leave it to the men's sense of discipline to give the stuff up—we had to search them. The popularity of General Dodds with the troops received a rude shock that day.

In the middle of the town there was a large square. On one side of this square there was an enormous building surrounded by high walls, having a gateway literally built of human skulls and bones. This was the king's palace, now a burnt-out ruin, and it was here that we took up our quarters.

The general issued a proclamation deposing King Behanzin, and announcing a French protectorate over the country. The dethroned king became a fugitive in the extreme north. He was not captured and deported until more than a year afterwards, but to all intents the campaign was now over.

"Ah!" said a French sergeant-major to me, "This fool of a Behanzin listened too much to the English and the Germans, who told him that the French were a people he could take all sorts of liberties with. He knows better now. They say that he has sent messengers to Lagos to ask the English to help him. If your countrymen are wise, my friend, they will mind their own business and leave us to mind ours."

The English government took the tip.

The expeditionary force, with the exception of a battalion of Senegalese and a company of the Legion, which were left behind as a garrison, started on its return to the coast on the 27th November. I didn't volunteer to remain behind, nor did Petrovski—we were both of opinion that we had seen as much of Dahomey as we wanted.

On Christmas Day, 1892, we embarked on the *Thibet*, a mixed crowd, thirteen hundred strong, consisting of legionaries, Marine Infantry, Senegalese Tirailleurs, Senegalese Spahis, sailors of the French West African squadron, and about a hundred Senegalese women and half as many children, the families of the Senegalese troops, whose wives and children always follow them, even in war time.

We arrived at Oran on January 11th in the night. There were 214 legionaries on board now, five having died on the voyage, and of these 214 no less than 69 had to be carried ashore, to the military hospital, on stretchers.

There was no public demonstration at Oran, for the arrival of the ship was unexpected; but there was a great fuss made of those of us who were well enough to proceed to the depot at Sidi-bel-Abbes. There were only about a hundred of us.

It was about seven o'clock in the evening when we arrived at Sidi-bel-Abbes, and we found the whole town illuminated in our honour. Waiting for us at the station were the band of the Legion, the town council, all the officers of the Legion then in Bel-Abbes, and a number of legionaries to act as torch-bearers, and other legionaries under arms to march on our flanks to prevent the crowd from hugging us to death.

After a sort of triumphal promenade round the town we were taken to the hall of the fencing society, where a banquet awaited us. There were some grandiloquent speeches about the glorious French army in general, and the extra-super glorious Foreign Legion in particular, and then we were escorted to barracks loaded down with presents of pipes, cigars, knives, and all sorts of useful and useless things.

Such was the finish of an eventful four months. Neither Petrovski nor myself had received a scratch, and, though we had suffered from many slight attacks of fever and dysentery, we had neither of us been struck off duty for a single day. If the casualty bill of the expedition be looked at it will be seen that we had been very fortunate indeed. Out of a force comprising only about 2,300 combatants we had lost in killed, 15 officers and 143 men; three officers and 90 men had died of sickness; and 27 officers and 344 men had been wounded. The total casualties, therefore, amounted to 27 *per cent*, of the strength. If the men incapacitated by sickness were added to this it would bring the casualties up to nearly 75 *per cent*, of the strength.

We were all medically examined on the following day, and any man who wanted to go was sent to the convalescent depot for three months to pick up; but neither my friend nor myself took advantage of this chance. We resumed duty at once, and within a month we were so "fed up "with the monotony of life at the depot that we would gladly have welcomed any chance of going on service again.

CHAPTER 23

With the Mounted Company at Ain-Sefra

We had not been back at Sidi-bel-Abbes long when a severe epidemic of typhoid fever broke out in the garrison. Seeing that the sanitary arrangements generally were of the most primitive description, it was a matter of wonder that typhoid was ever absent. Poor Petrovski was one of the first struck down, and he was still very ill when I was transferred to a battalion under orders to garrison Ain-Sefra, a post on the edge of the Great Sahara on the one side, and close to the Moroccan border on the other.

The march to Ain-Sefra was a three weeks' job. We started every morning at two o'clock and kept on, with a halt of ten minutes in every hour, until eleven, when the order to pitch camp would be given. In a few minutes from then our little shelter tents would be found pitched in regular straight lines; the camp kettles would be on the fires; and the legionaries would be busy cleaning their arms and equipment for the morrow so as to be free to lie down immediately after the meal. It was pretty hard work to march something like twenty-five miles day after day with about eighty pounds on one's back, and for the first few days the knapsack straps galled the shoulders terribly, the cartridge pouches caused a permanent dull ache in the abdomen, and the perspiration chafed the soft parts of the body to soreness; but after the first week we trudged along as merry as grigs, laughing, singing and smoking as if we were simply out for a pleasurable stroll. When we came to a village or a town we straightened ourselves up, the bugles blared out a stirring march, and we stepped out jauntily, as if we would say: "Yes, we are the Legion! Look at us! We don't feel the weight on our backs, and the further we march the better we like it."

All the same, I don't think that there was a man among us who wanted any more of it when we at last got to our destination. The legionary is the best marching soldier in the wide world, and he knows it; but he doesn't love marching, for all that.

At Ain-Sefra I was posted to the mounted company. This company was not cavalry—we were simply infantrymen mounted on mules in order to enable us to get over the long distances we had to traverse in patrolling the Moroccan border or hunting marauding Arabs in the desert to the south of us. We were kept pretty hard at work, and as we were continually having brushes with somebody it was more or less like campaigning in a mild sort of way.

On one occasion we were within an ace of being wiped out to a man. A band of Touaregs—a white race of Mahomedans, whose headquarters are in Timbuktoo, and who are marauders by profession—was reported to be holding one of the oases to the south of us, and we were sent to persuade them to shift. We were still a long way from our destination, and had encamped for the night without any idea that our quarry would be bold enough to come so far to attack us without waiting for us to attack them. As sometimes happens when it is considered that a force is in no danger of attack, we were careless—our sentries nodded on their posts, and we had no outlying piquets out. About an hour before sunrise the camp was roused by the report of a rifle fired some distance away out in the desert. We had just time to seize our arms and form up when we found that the Touaregs were upon us. We had no difficulty in repelling the attack; but if that, presumably accidental, discharge of the Touareg rifle had not occurred we would certainly have been surprised in our sleep and probably massacred to a man. Over-confidence is both a military virtue and a military fault—it is a variety of swelled head that the legion suffers from badly.

After two or three months of the mounted company I was recalled to Sidi-bel-Abbes and promoted to be sergeant-major.

I found when I returned to the depot that Petrovski had already been promoted, having got over his bout of fever.

I rather think that our promotion was a bait to get us to extend our service, for the colonel sent for both of us and point-blank asked us if we would re-engage to serve another five years. At that time a non-commissioned officer, not a private, re-engaging for the Legion was given the bounty offered to an ordinary French soldier. That was the handsome sum of two thousand six hundred *francs*—£104—of which six hundred *francs*—£24—was paid to him at once, and interest paid on the remainder till his final discharge, when the principal was handed over. The colonel pointed this out, but he did it in such a way as suggested delicately that he didn't think that the money argument would have much influence with us. He harped more strongly on the string that if we could see our way to become naturalised Frenchmen a glorious career was open to us—we could go to the college of Saint-Maixent, and from there obtain commissions, as Frenchmen, either in the Legion or in the Marine Infantry.

The prospect would have appealed to me if it had not been for the naturalisation proviso. I did not want to part with the nationality to which I was born, and so, "in spite of all temptation to belong to another nation, I remained an Englishman," as "Pinafore" has it.

There is nothing more to tell. In due time Petrovski and I found ourselves back in Marseilles, having dinner in the very hotel where, five years before, we had the row with the French officers.

"Well," said I to my friend, "have you any regrets?"

"None—I would do the like today, in the same circumstances," he replied, as he puffed meditatively at his cigar. "The Legion has done much for us, my friends; but it is not so kind to everyone."

"That is so," I replied. "*Vive la Legion! Vive la France!*"

CHAPTER 24

Insanity in the Legion

A great deal of nonsense has been written about the life in the Legion being of a sort that drives men to madness, and the number of men invalided out of the corps on account of insanity is pointed to as proof of the assertion. I am not going to assert that the percentage of insane men in the legion is not greater than in any other armed force; but I do say that, if it is so, a better reason can be found for it than the hardness of the life. A large proportion of legionaries are eccentric—if they were not so they would not be in the Legion at all—and a good many are distinctly "queer in the upper storey"; but almost without exception they were so when they enlisted, and the Legion is in no way responsible for their condition.

It is inevitable that the mental balance of a certain number of these men will become more and more tilted until the border-line between eccentricity and insanity is passed, and I think the fact that so few, comparatively speaking, do pass this line is a strong argument that the Legion really cures diseased minds rather than causes them. Looking backward, I would not like to be positive that I was perfectly sane myself when I joined, but I don't think that there can be any doubt as to my sanity a few months afterwards. I have known many men who were morose, unsociable, and continually brooding when they joined, but who afterwards became cheerful, companionable, and even gay under the influence of the mind-anodyne that life in the Legion, in my opinion, provides for the mentally distressed.

As to the "*cafard*," or "*soudanite*," as the doctors call it—a form of mania supposed to be peculiar to the Legion—it is nothing more nor less, according to my idea of it, than a sort of hysteria set up by the action of a monotonous routine upon restless active natures in that climate. It is nature calling out insistently for change. It is but rarely that manifestations of the "*cafard*" end in tragedy—in ninety-nine cases out of a hundred they simply assume the character of an ordinary drunken quarrel or an extraordinary drunken spree.

It is common enough to hear British soldiers on foreign service, and especially in India, declare that they are "fed-up" and feel as if they must do something desperate. Those British soldiers have the "*cafard*"; but they have no suspicion that they are afflicted with the "terrible" madness of the French Foreign Legion, and they will perhaps be very much surprised to learn it from me.

The pranks played by legionaries when taken by "*cafard*" range between tragedy and farce, seldom touching either extremity, but being, for the most part, about midway between the two. I will give a few instances to illustrate the diversity of their character:—

There was a sergeant, employed as clerk in the regimental office at Sidi-bel-Abbes, who had once upon a time been an officer in the regular French army; but he had "come a mucker," and had enlisted in the Legion as a Belgian. One day the colonel happened to be confined to bed and was visited in his lodgings by the sergeant-clerk, who had some papers for the chief's signature. The colonel happened to be asleep when the sergeant arrived, and the non-commissioned officer was shown into the dressing-room to await the moment when the commanding officer should awake. Here the sight of the colonel's uniform coat gave the sergeant the idea that it would vary the monotony a little if he took a stroll round the town and showed the legionaries their colonel in a new light—it was dark and the colonel was sick, so nobody would be surprised at his muffling up his face.

Half-an-hour afterwards a sergeant of the Legion, strolling along the tree-shaded Rue de Mascara, saw in the gloom the five-striped sleeve of the colonel's coat just in front of him, and braced himself up to justify his reputation as one of the smartest non-commissioned officers of the corps. His salute did not appear to please his commanding officer this time, however, for the five-*galonned* sleeve was raised in an imperative signal to stop, and an angry voice, which the sergeant would not have recognised for that of the colonel if it had not been accompanied by the five-striped sleeve aforesaid, ordered him to return to barracks at once and take four days' arrest for slouching about the town in a dirty uniform and saluting his colonel in an unsoldier-like manner.

The poor sergeant was struck dumb. He, one of the dandies of the Legion, and a man who prided himself on walking as if he had a rifle barrel for a spine, to be accused of "slouching" and wearing a dirty uniform! His feelings had been mortally wounded. His chin sank, and as he dejectedly moved off all the starch seemed to have been taken out of him and he did "slouch."

The "colonel" passed on and promenaded the town for an hour, dealing out four days' arrest and speaking injurious words to every non-commissioned officer he met who was vain of his soldierlike appearance, donating unasked favours and bestowing paternal benedictions on scallywags of legionaries, making amiable salutations to ladies of a class that the real colonel was very much "down on," and behaving generally in a way that horrified the respectable people who saw him.

If he had stopped there and had managed to get the uniform off and replaced without discovery, it would have been very hard lines on the rightful owner of the clothes, for the poor colonel would never have been able to live down the scandal; but he must needs vary the proceedings by going into a low-class *café* where surely an officer of even the most junior rank had never been seen before, and fraternising with some legionaries he found there. Here he could not escape recognition, and the glee of the legionaries at the joke attained such proportions that the proprietor of the cafe grew seriously alarmed, and appealed to a couple of officers who happened to be passing to take their colonel away, as he was very drunk and was creating a disturbance.

In another case two legionaries disappeared for a week and then marched gravely into barracks, got up after the style of grenadiers of the eighteenth century: tall, mitre-like headdresses, blue *coatees*, red waistcoats, white knee-breeches and long blue-cloth gaiters. They had been for a promenade in the desert, and with a great deal of ingenuity and no little sartorial skill had fashioned these archaic uniforms out of their own.

Two other legionaries, both of them ex-officers of the Austrian army, marched off southward one morning with their kits on their backs and their arms in their hands. On being brought back and charged with attempted desertion, they indignantly denied any intention to desert, and when asked to explain their proceedings on any other hypothesis, coolly said that they had enlisted to fight and as the authorities had not carried out their contract by providing them with fighting, they went out to find some for themselves.

The "*cafard*" took a Belgian, said to have been once an inspector of

155

police, in a peculiar way: he committed burglaries and picked pockets for the mere sake of the excitement involved. He certainly did not steal for profit, because he invariably returned his plunder after getting clear off with it, as was proved when he was at last taken in the act of burgling a house in the town.

In one case I know of a tragical termination to a case of *"cafard"* was avoided by the presence of mind and pluck of the intended victim. There was a captain in the Legion, one of many officers who had risen from the ranks, who, like most rankers, knew too much for his sergeant-major's comfort, and he used to get very much on that non-commissioned officer's nerves. Things came to a climax at a time when the company was on the march. One afternoon when they had halted for the day and the camp had been pitched, the captain bowled the sergeant-major out in some little "try-on" or other liberty that non-commissioned officers attempt with success on commissioned officers who are not up to all the moves of the game, and spoke to him very sharply.

The petty worries incidental to the position of company-sergeant-major are much intensified when the company is on the march, and this particular sergeant-major's nerves were very much out of tune when the captain started to rag him. The result of the ragging was that the nerves could stand no more—the sergeant-major got *"cafard."* He rushed to his tent, got his revolver, and announced his intention of making a vacancy for a captain at once. Several of the men ran to warn the officer to get out of the way until the sergeant-major could be secured; but the captain was not one of the sort that gets out of the way. Instead of doing that he went straight up to the sergeant-major and said: "I hear that you want to kill me, sergeant-major. If that is so you had better come along to my tent—I would much rather you'd do it there than out here."

The would-be murderer had raised his revolver on seeing the captain approach, but the officer had airily waved it aside, and the sergeant-major had listened to him with the pistol still raised, but without attempting to fire. As soon as the officer had ceased speaking he turned his back on the man who wanted to kill him and strolled off towards his tent, as if expecting the sergeant- major to follow him as a matter of course.

And the sergeant-major did follow, seemingly as if it were the only thing to do.

When they arrived at the officer's tent the captain invited the sergeant-major to put the revolver down while he explained his reasons for wanting to use it on his captain; and so ingrained was the habit of obedience to the officer's commands that the sergeant-major did this without protest.

The captain promptly picked up the firearm and drew the cartridges.

"Now I think you had better lie down here for an hour or so," he said sympathetically to the sergeant-major. "It won't do for the men to see you again in that state."

And that was the end of the incident, for the captain magnanimously recognised that some of the blame belonged to him, and took no steps to have the sergeant-major punished. Magnanimity of this sort is not a military virtue, for to let men who have committed serious offences go unpunished is the surest way of destroying discipline, but it is common enough in the legion, and in this curiously contradictory force it seems to have a beneficial effect on discipline instead of loosening its bonds.

It is common enough, too—in fact, it is the most common manifestation of the "*cafard*"—to hear legionaries howling opprobrious names at their officers and making other derogatory remarks, but it is very seldom indeed that this abuse is "heard "by those affected by it.

To finish the chapter, I will give an instance of the tragical side of the "*cafard*." This occurred in one of the small garrisons in the south of Oran, and the principal actor was a Swiss legionary. One day this legionary sallied forth in search of adventure, taking with him his rifle and sixty rounds of ammunition. Having helped himself to food and other things in an Arab village, he was pursued by the men belonging to the "*douar*" and by some gendarmes who had been called in to arrest the thief. They overtook and surrounded the legionary, but were unable to arrest him as he showed fight, killing an Arab and wounding a gendarme.

Next morning a detachment of the Legion and some *spahis* arrived upon the scene, and found that the mutineer had entrenched himself and was prepared to fight the lot of them. His kepi was seen to be sticking up above the crest of the redoubt the man had built to shelter him, and a hot fire was opened on it. The man was not in its neighbourhood, though, and the fire failed to harm him. On the other side of the account he killed three of the assailants and would undoubtedly have bagged many more had it not been for a resourceful corporal of the Legion, who made a wide detour and came up behind him without his being aware of the presence of an enemy until the very instant when the corporal jumped on his back.

When examined by the commandant of the detachment the Swiss said simply: "Don't worry me. I was nearly dead with *ennui*, and I had to find some distraction."

Strange to say, this man, although sentenced to death, was not executed, although it was admitted that he was not insane.

CHAPTER 25

Queer Fish

Some queer fish find their way into the net that recruits the Legion. In this chapter I give sketches of a few of this sort of legionary, but it must not be assumed that they are fair samples of the mass of legionaries. The average legionary is a working-class man who has probably deserted from some other regiment in the French army, enlisting in the legion as a Belgian or a Swiss, or from a foreign army, and men of superior position and education who have made a mess of their lives are, after all, merely exceptions, though there are a great many of them. Further, I did not myself come across all, or even most of the men I here write of, but have culled the accounts from tradition and accounts of the Legion by various writers.

Many people who read the foreign news in the columns of our daily newspapers may remember the case of a German lieutenant of artillery named Kauffmann. He had a quarrel with one of his comrades in the street, drew his sword and wounded him. The injured man was carried into barracks, and actually while the doctor was attending to him Kauffmann returned, placed a revolver to the wounded man's head and blew out his brains. Kauffmann then escaped and enlisted in the Legion. As the French Government will surrender a murderer who enlists in the Legion, though no other sort of criminal is said to be given up—a statement, by the way, which I doubt, as there are such things as extradition treaties—Kauffmann was not apparently very wise in doing this, as the German Government knew perfectly well where to find him. The German Government, however, did not claim him, and he was in due course sent to Tonkin, where I fancy he died.

An officer of a vastly different stamp who deserted from the German army I knew very well. He was an Alsatian and his family was rich. In due course he became an officer in a German Lancers regiment, though his sympathies and the sympathies of his family were wholly French. In due course, also, he fell in love, and the sympathies of the girl he fell in love with were French also—French to the extent that she declared she could not marry a man who wore the German uniform. He had only donned the uniform himself because he was obliged to do it in some shape or form, and he liked the wearing of it as little as the girl did. So, with the girl's full concurrence, and probably at her instigation, he deserted from his German regiment and enlisted in the Legion, with the idea of gaining a commission under the tricolour. He was not at all reticent about his affairs, being probably vain of his sentimental attachment to the French flag, so I came to know a great deal about his career.

Years afterwards I read René Bazin's fine novel, *Les Oberlé*, which had not been written when I knew the man I am writing of, and found that some of the incidents in the book agreed almost exactly with incidents in his career related to me by the Uhlan deserter. Either the arm of coincidence must have been much longer than usual or the novel was written round my friend's case. Whether he got the commission or not I do not know. He could have entered the Legion as a sub-lieutenant at first, I imagine, if he had known the way to go about it.

I met many Alsatians and Lorraines who took no pains to conceal their hatred of Germany, and things German, and I have no doubt whatever that sentiment of that sort is at the bottom of most of the enlistments into the Legion from the conquered provinces.

A very different sentimental reason for joining the Legion was given to the colonel one day when he was inspecting a batch of recruits. He came to a man with a fine intelligent face—a man who looked anything but a soldier in his bearing—and, his curiosity piqued, asked the recruit what profession he followed prior to enlistment.

"I was professor in such a college at Geneva," replied the "blue."

"Then what did you come here for, in the name of all that's wonderful?" asked the colonel.

"I found out that I am fond of war, *mon colonel.*"

Wasn't this a case of "*cafard*" in a college professor?

The story goes that there was once an ex-bishop in the Legion. I heard it while I was in the Legion, as a regimental legend, but it was only after I had left that I saw the story in full in a French paper: A French force in Mexico had taken a small town, and the general in command, wishing to show the shy inhabitants that the French were

Christians like themselves, and not savages as they were represented to be, decided to have a parade celebration of High Mass. In order to make the service as imposing as possible the troops were set to decorate the church with palms and flowers, officers and men put on their full uniforms, and the drummers and buglers were placed so that they could beat and sound the salute at the elevation of the Host. When all was ready no priest could be found the *cure* of the parish had run away, and the monks of a neighbouring monastery refused to open their gate or to hold any communication with the conqueror. The general was on the point of renouncing the service and ordering the men to be marched away when the sentry on the church door presented arms as the general passed, and asked permission to speak to him.

"What do you want?" said the colonel.

"I was thinking, *mon general*, that if you cannot find a priest to perform the functions of the Mass I could do it just as well."

"You! What do you mean?"

"I mean," replied the legionary, "that before I became a soldier I was a bishop, and that, never having been unfrocked, I am a priest still."

After questioning the legionary further the general consented to his performing the service. Putting on the sacred vestments that were found in the vestry, and with the assistance of a lieutenant as an acolyte, the legionary performed the service of the Mass with perfect dignity, and the inhabitants were reassured as the general had hoped they would be. This ex-bishop was said to have been such a good fighter that he was decorated for exceptional bravery during the campaign.

Another priest in the Legion exercised his religious functions in Tunis, according to a French paper. It was at the time of the Fashoda incident, when the French garrisons in Tunis were strengthened, that a legionary was drowned at Zarzis while attempting to save a fisherman whose boat had capsized. The dead man's comrades fashioned him a coffin out of packing-cases, the boards retaining the original inscriptions, one of which was: "KEEP THE CONTENTS DRY." No priest was available in the ordinary way, but an Italian legionary stepped out of the ranks, and, announcing that he was a priest, proceeded to recite the committal service from memory, which was, perhaps, a pretty fair proof of his assertion.

Whether or no I myself served with any ex-priests or ex-ministers of religion, I am unable to say. I knew more than one or two legionaries, whom I suspected of having been something of the sort; but legionaries with a past seldom or never talk about it, and those whose past life becomes known have not made it known themselves, but have been the victims of some accident or other.

When I came back from Dahomey there was, in the company I was posted to, a man who could not have been less than forty years of age, and was probably older. He made no friends and hardly ever spoke to any one unless directly addressed, but when he did speak he was always polite, and he was very considerate in his behaviour towards his comrades. His uncommunicativeness was patently not due to moroseness or melancholy it seemed to be due to the fact that he lived in a continual dream. He was undoubtedly a man of superior position, and I early formed the opinion that he had been an officer, but nobody had any notion of his real identity until he was killed in Tonkin some year or two after I had left the Legion, when it was discovered that he was a German nobleman, the son of a general, and himself an ex-officer of the German army. What caused the break in his life I never heard.

Of Englishmen in the Legion I don't think I met more than a dozen in the whole course of my service. I imagine that all of them, with the exception of two, had served in the British army, but I only received any confidences from two of them, and these two wanted my assistance as interpreter as they did not speak any language but their own. They had both of them been private soldiers in the British army, and I am afraid they never got beyond that rank in the Legion, though what became of them I have no idea. Of the others, three to my knowledge died of typhoid at Bel-Abbes, two deserted and were not afterwards heard of, and one was a sergeant when I left.

None of the Englishmen I met appealed to me as possible friends, and my acquaintance with them was limited to an occasional chance meeting, when we would exchange some such remark as "How would you like to be in Piccadilly just now?" or, "I think Aldershot is better than this." I have no doubt that if I had been closely associated with an Englishman in my daily work, I would have got on more familiar terms; but I never had one, to my knowledge, in the same company with me. An abstract of nationalities that I once saw in the regimental office at Bel-Abbes gave the number of Englishmen serving in the Legion as 51, and of Americans as 28. If that was so I cannot imagine where they were stowed away, for I never met more of my own countrymen than I have stated, and of Americans I never came across more than two.

I think the saddest case of a legionary with a past that I ever heard of concerned a Frenchman. He was a graduate of the *Ecole Polytechnique*, and commenced his career in the diplomatic service, being an *attaché* at the French Embassies at Stockholm and The Hague. Then he was made a *sous-préfet* in France, and during the war with Germany was employed as an auxiliary to the General Staff, and made himself so useful that he was rewarded with the Cross of the Legion of Honour. Then he entered the regular army as an officer, but soon resigned and was lost sight of for some years until he turned up as a soldier of the Foreign Legion. He so distinguished himself in the legion that he was given a commission after only two years' service—and a year afterwards was cashiered for disgraceful conduct of an unmentionable sort.

Another sad case of a Frenchman who enlisted as a foreigner was that of a barrister. This man, after completing his compulsory period of service in the French regular army, voluntarily remained on to complete the period of service necessary to qualify him for an officer's commission in the reserve. During this extra period things did not go smoothly with him, for he got into trouble and was sent to Algeria to serve in the "Zephyrs," as the penal battalions are called. His time finished, he returned to Paris and ran through a fortune which had been left to him during his absence. He then turned his attention to writing and did well at it, but the restlessness of Algeria had got hold of him, and he enlisted in the Legion. Arrived in Algeria it was not long before he pined to be in Paris again, and he deserted. Some little time afterwards, being then clad in rags and tatters and bearing other signs of the most abject want, he touched an old friend on the shoulder in a Paris street and begged for money to carry him to Spain.

The friend was a man of some public position, and it would have been something of a scandal if he had been found out in assisting a deserter, but he listened to the request nevertheless, and not only paid the passage to Spain, and gave the deserter money to start him when he got there, but accompanied him to Havre and saw him on board the boat. But before the boat started the intending emigrant managed to pick a quarrel with a custom-house officer and was hauled off to the police-station for creating a disturbance. Here it was discovered that he was a deserter from the Foreign Legion, and he was handed over to the military authorities, who sent him back to Algeria. After serving the imprisonment awarded for the desertion he seized the first opportunity that presented itself to desert again, and was probably killed or reduced to slavery by one of the wild tribes of Morocco, for he was never heard of again.

A more cheerful story is connected with the name of a lieutenant of the Legion named Eblit. He had been an officer in the French regular army and had resigned his commission in order to get married and go into business with his brother-in-law; but the business didn't prosper, and he suspected his wife of betraying him, so he disappeared and enlisted into the Legion as a foreigner under a false name. One day in Tonkin General de Negrier was inspecting a detachment of the Legion and stopped before Legionary X.

"What is your name?" asked the general, looking the legionary straight in the eyes.

"X——, *mon general.*"

The general passed on, but after going a few paces he returned brusquely.

"I don't think that your name is X——," he said, "and I don't believe that you are a Belgian. I think you are someone I used to know very well. If you are that man you have nothing to be ashamed of that I know. Will you tell me your real name, and why you have abandoned it?"

"You are right, *mon general,*" replied the legionary. "My real name is Eblit, and I was once a lieutenant in the battalion you commanded. I have no interests now in civil life, and I enlisted in the Legion to see if I could regain a commission. I enlisted in a false name because I did not wish any one to know that I had been an officer."

General de Negrier made Eblit a sergeant on the spot, and eight days afterwards he was seriously wounded. For his gallantry on this occasion he was given a commission. He was invalided to Algeria with his wound, but was back in Tonkin and fighting again before three months had passed.

The fate of another ex-officer of the French army was not so happy. He was obliged to resign his commission for private reasons, and sank down to the very depths of misery. Then he joined the Legion, and in course of time became a sergeant, but had small prospect of getting any further, as he was given to drink. He was treated with the greatest forbearance and consideration by the officers or he could never have retained the rank he had, but he went from bad to worse and eventually cut his throat in a paroxysm of self-reproach.

On one occasion the inspecting general at a parade at Sidi-bel-Abbes stopped as he was passing along the ranks, and shook hands with a legionary standing in the ranks. The story went that the legionary, who was generally suspected of having been "somebody," was an old comrade of the general's who had been obliged to disappear from France owing to being mixed up in a terrible scandal. Such a thing was likely enough, for the scandals that lie buried in the Legion are many, but the general's reason for shaking hands might have had nothing whatever to do with the legionary's previous life. What lent probability to the story was the fact that the legionary absolutely refused to satisfy his comrades' curiosity as to his previous acquaintance with the general.

An ex-officer of the French army, whose past was no secret, joined at Sidi-bel-Abbes some little time before I left. He was at that time well over forty, I imagine, and was hardly to be described as a good soldier either on parade or off—as far as life in barracks was concerned. What he was like in the firing line I don't know, for I was never on active service with him. He had aforetime risen from the ranks in the regular French army, having passed through the non-commissioned officers' college of Saint-Maixent, and after about half-a-dozen years' service as an officer had resigned his commission to take service in the army of one of the South American republics. Then he joined the insurgent forces in another South American state, was captured by the Government troops, and was condemned to death. He escaped and made his way to Paris, where he found himself "down on his uppers," and enlisted in the Legion. He was still serving as a private of the second-class when I left the Legion, and I don't know what eventually became of him.

I could give many more instances of ex-officers of the French army serving in the Legion, but I have given sufficient, I think, to show that the Legion is the refuge of many men of that class. There are many ex-officers of foreign armies in the Legion, too, but in my opinion the French ex-officers outnumber the total of all armies by at least two to one.

Among foreign ex-officers in the Legion was a certain Kewitch, who had been a lieutenant of Austrian artillery. After serving with credit in Tonkin, where he was employed in making military sketches of the country, he returned to Sidi-bel-Abbes, where, tiring of the monotony, he persuaded a squad of twelve men to desert with him. They took their arms and their kits with them and marched through the country in military order; but this did not prevent their being ignominiously brought back by the *gendarmes*. Kewitch got thirty days in prison for his share in the freak, and this was very lenient treatment indeed. At the end of it he was sent back to Tonkin at his own request in order that he might settle down there as a colonist when his time was completed.

An ex-lieutenant of the German army, named Von der Goltz, nephew of the general of the same name, did not get off so easily, as he was tried by court-martial and got two years' imprisonment for refusing to do punishment drill awarded for two days' illegal absence.

A lieutenant of Hungarian cavalry, serving in a regiment of which his father was colonel, was drawn into a row with a German at a *café chantant*. A duel resulted, and the German was killed. The lieutenant was banished from Austria for three years, and his father ordered him to enlist in the Legion. The youngster was a good fellow and an excellent soldier, so his exile to the Legion did not weigh very hardly on him. He went to Tonkin, behaved well there, and became a sergeant in a very short time.

I have heard of a corporal of the Legion who had been a colonel of Austrian engineers, of another Austrian who in happier times was secretary of the Austro-Hungarian embassy at Rome, of an Italian who had forfeited the rank of colonel in his own country, and who was recognised by a general as having formerly been military *attaché* of the Italian embassy at an important foreign court, and of many, very many, other men of many nations who found refuge and oblivion in the Legion after lapses of sorts; but I will not go into details of any of these cases, for I have written enough of this class of legionary.

As might be expected, there are many men of the very lowest class of society in the Legion also, but the corps is no more mainly composed of them than it is of broken men of good position. The bulk of the legionaries are just men of the class that would fill the ranks of a voluntary armed force in any country, and the majority of them are drawn to the Legion by the glamour and romance that surrounds its glorious flag.

The Legion is a mercenary force, but it is mercenary in theory only, for the pay of the legionary is so utterly contemptible as to be no pay at all. Those of the Legion's detractors who say that the legionary fights and works for nothing are stating but the bare truth. It is impossible for a private soldier at the depot of the Legion to live any life but a life of rigid self-denial if he cannot in some way supplement the wretched halfpenny a day, which is all the cash he gets. In Tonkin the soldier is in a slightly better position, but even there, with the extra allowances, his pay will not find him in a moderate quantity of drink and tobacco. That the soldiers of the Legion fight in the splendid manner peculiar to them, for practically their bare board and lodging, stamps them as being the most extraordinary mercenary soldiers that ever existed, even if there is nothing else to give them a claim to priority among mercenaries. It is a scandal that France should take so much from these gallant men and give them so little in return.

CHAPTER 26

Conclusion

"What is the Foreign Legion?" I was once asked by a man who passed for being well-informed on most subjects. Wondering mildly at his ignorance I was about to enlighten him when he opened his mouth again and paralysed me by asking further: "Is it the same as the Legion of Honour?"

The remembrance of this question has put it into my head that there may be, even now, a great many people who will read this book who would like to know something more about the history and constitution of the Legion than can be gathered from the preceding pages.

The French Foreign Legion, then, is the descendant of the Scottish Archers employed by Charles VII. of France, and of the Swiss, the Albanians, the Flemings, the Walloons, the Lasquenets (who were Germans, by the way), the Irish, the Italians, the Swedes, the English, and the Spanish Guards employed by his successors. The French have always been sweet on getting foreigners to help them in fighting their battles and guarding their kings.

At the revolution of 1793 the Convention asked the aid of all the European peoples, and the result of this appeal was the formation of several foreign regiments in the revolutionary army.

Under the Empire there were in the French army regiments composed of Swiss, Poles, Hanoverians, Irish, Portuguese, Spaniards, Albanians, Greeks, Croats, and Prussians.

After the fall of Napoleon all these foreign regiments were disbanded, but Louis XVIII. created the Royal Foreign legion in their place. This foreign regiment became merged into the regular French army and gradually lost its distinctive character—its present representative is the 86th Regiment of the line—and there was no real foreign regiment in French service again until after the revolution of 1830. On May 9th, 1831, the French Chambers decreed the formation of a Foreign Legion which was not to be employed on the soil of France. This force consisted of seven battalions of eight companies each, and the men were distributed by nationalities, the 1st, 2nd, and 3rd Battalions consisting of Swiss and Germans, the 4th Battalion was composed of Spaniards, the 5th of Italians, the 6th of Dutchmen and Belgians, and the 7th of Poles. It was very soon found that this separation of nationalities would not work, for the different battalions took to fighting among themselves, and the present plan mixing up all nationalities indiscriminately in the same company was adopted.

In my time in the Legion, and I do not think the constitution has since been changed, the Legion consisted of ten battalions of four companies each, the strength of a company being from 250 to 300 men. These ten battalions were divided into two regiments, the head quarters of the 1st Regiment being at Sidi-bel-Abbes and that of the 2nd Regiment at Saida. The whole strength of the Legion in Algeria was quartered in the province of Oran, there being no stations for legionaries either in the province of Constantine or the province of Algiers. Two battalions of each regiment were stationed in Tonkin, and the wastage in these four battalions was so great that drafts amounting in the aggregate to the strength of a battalion had to be sent out to them every year.

The depot companies were often very unwieldy, as they had no fixed establishment, and sometimes contained more men in each of them than the strength of a battalion—indeed, a depot company has been known to contain more than 4,000 men. Notwithstanding this elasticity, a depot company has only the same number of officers and non-commissioned officers as a service company, and as a necessary consequence recruits are not looked after and supervised in the way that is necessary to the proper education of a recruit. Things generally are badly managed at Sidi-bel-Abbes, or were so in my time, and no man whose experience has been solely gained there is competent to form an opinion about life in the Legion that it is worth any one's while to read—the real Legion, and the naked legionary, are only to be studied on active service, and the depot wallah knows nothing whatever about one or the other.

It is very difficult to arrive at any reliable estimate of the percentages of the different nationalities that go to make up the personnel of the Legion, for even official returns are not to be depended upon, as a great many men give nationalities other than their own when joining.

To illustrate the great discrepancy between estimates I will take one from a French and one from a German source and compare them. Let us take the estimate of the number of Frenchmen first: The French estimate gives the number of actual Frenchmen in the Legion as one-half of the total, and the number of Alsatians and Lorraines at 55 *per cent*, of the remainder, leaving only about twenty-five *per cent*, of the legionaries to all other nationalities. In the German estimate France is only credited with providing 8 *per cent*, of the legionaries. This estimate is manifestly absurd.

It might possibly have been near the truth before 1881, when Frenchmen could only get into the Legion by representing themselves as Belgians or Swiss, but a law was passed in October, 1881, allowing a Frenchman to enlist in the Legion provided that he had previously completed his period of compulsory service in an ordinary regiment and produced his "military small-book," evidence that he had never been convicted of an offence that debarred him from military service, and a certificate of identity. This law is now taken advantage of by numbers of adventurous Frenchmen, and quite as many more, who are ineligible under the decree, get in by the old dodge of adopting some other nationality, which relieves them of the necessity of producing any papers at all, or, in fact, giving any account of themselves.

My idea is that the truth is something between the two estimates. When I was in the Legion I think that quite half the men I came into contact with were either pure French or men from Alsace and Lorraine with French sympathies. The German estimate says that 52 *per cent*, of the legionaries are fond of "*Gott* knows vot in vinegar, und dooce knows vot in rum," while the French credits the Fatherland with only providing 10 *per cent.*, and howling about it as if every legionary was made in Germany. Here again I think the truth is something betwixt and between. There are a great many Germans in the Legion—I have an idea that both Petrovski and myself owed our quick promotion to this fact, for our knowledge of the language was useful—and I think the percentage is nearer 25 than 10 *per cent.*

Both estimates agree in crediting England with ½ per cent. This would give about sixty Britishers for the whole Legion, and all I can say about this is that I don't believe that there were ever as many as sixty natives of these islands in the Legion at one time. The two estimates agree very well about the remaining nationalities, too, both giving the highest percentage, after French and Germans, to Italians. Then, in order, come Belgians, Swiss, Spaniards, Austrians, Russians, Turks, Slavs, Greeks, and Poles. Of all the nations named only two— Russia and Turkey—are credited with as low a percentage as 1 *per cent.*, and England comes last, with ½ *per cent*, of all the nations named in either list. Americans are not given a place in either list, the French estimate having a note to the effect that Americans are not to be found in the Legion at all. This is certainly not the truth, for there are Americans in the Legion, though very few.

The ages of the legionaries cover a very wide range. It is pretty safe to say that almost every recruit who gives the minimum age of eighteen on enlistment is younger, and that almost every one of those who give ages of from thirty-five to forty are older, so that it is no exaggeration to say that the ranks of the Legion include men of all ages from 16 to 55. An English officer would scout the idea of sending a private soldier of 55 on active service, and would probably not admit that a man of that age would be of much use for the duties of a territorial soldier.

Our military authorities hold that a man of thirty-five is too old for the lowest class of the Army Reserve, yet there are thousands of men of and above that age serving in the Foreign Legion, fighting better, marching better, and standing hardship better than their comrades of the ages that the British consider most suitable for active service. Young men of from 18 to 25 years of age do not stand hardship so well, and are not nearly so steady under fire, as older men; but the British War Office cannot be brought to see it. Our short service system must go on, I imagine, because it is necessary that the Army Reserve should be fed, but it is not easy to understand why the proportion of soldiers allowed to extend their service to qualify for pension has been cut down until we have practically no stiffening of old soldiers at all.

What is the military value of the Foreign Legion? Frankly, I think it is the finest fighting force the world has ever seen. Its value to France is not, however, to be measured by its value as a fighting force. The prestige of the Legion is so great with the ordinary French soldier that it occupies much the same position in the French army of today as the famous Old Guard occupied in the army of Napoleon, and the presence of a battalion of the Legion among a force of ordinary French troops will convince every soldier in that force that he is on the winning side. A man or a regiment that can hearten up a force to that extent would be of incalculable military value even if they never fired a shot.

Read what General de Negrier said of the legion: "…. *seul avec un regiment françgais je ne sors pas deux heures de la ville—avec une compagnie de la legion je fais le tour de Tonkin*" (with a French regiment I could not go two hours' journey from the town, but with a company of the Legion I could make the tour of Tonkin). After that, to write anything further as to the military value of the Legion would be descending to bathos.

Would I advise Englishmen to join the legion? No, I would not give any advice one way or the other. I myself am something of an optimist, and I had, moreover, seen much hard soldiering and had led an adventurous life in other ways before I dreamed of joining the Legion. It is quite possible, then, that my point of view was exceptionally favourable to seeing rose-colour where an ordinary man would only see dirty drab. My advice, then, would be to take a liberal discount off this account of mine to neutralise my optimism, and my Francophilism also if you like, and then judge for yourself. If you are thinking of committing suicide it will do you no harm to try the Legion first—it may possibly introduce you to a zest of life—that you have never felt, and in any case you can commit suicide just as well in Algeria, you know, as you can in London.

"The Legion of the Lost Ones" has enabled many and many a man to find himself, and it may perform the same service for you.

Partout où nous sommes passés,
Partout où nous sommes tombés,
Nous avons semé de la gloire,
Rataplan!
          (Old Chant of the Legion.)

LEONAUR

ALSO FROM LEONAUR

AVAILABLE IN SOFTCOVER OR HARDCOVER WITH DUST JACKET

LEONAUR

ALSO FROM LEONAUR
AVAILABLE IN SOFTCOVER OR HARDCOVER WITH DUST JACKET

FARAWAY CAMPAIGN *by F. James*—Experiences of an Indian Army Cavalry Officer in Persia & Russia During the Great War.

REVOLT IN THE DESERT *by T. E. Lawrence*—An account of the experiences of one remarkable British officer's war from his own perspective.

MACHINE-GUN SQUADRON *by A. M. G.*—The 20th Machine Gunners from British Yeomanry Regiments in the Middle East Campaign of the First World War.

A GUNNER'S CRUSADE *by Antony Bluett*—The Campaign in the Desert, Palestine & Syria as Experienced by the Honourable Artillery Company During the Great War .

DESPATCH RIDER *by W. H. L. Watson*—The Experiences of a British Army Motorcycle Despatch Rider During the Opening Battles of the Great War in Europe.

TIGERS ALONG THE TIGRIS *by E. J. Thompson*—The Leicestershire Regiment in Mesopotamia During the First World War.

HEARTS & DRAGONS *by Charles R. M. F. Crutwell*—The 4th Royal Berkshire Regiment in France and Italy During the Great War, 1914-1918.

INFANTRY BRIGADE: 1914 *by John Ward*—The Diary of a Commander of the 15th Infantry Brigade, 5th Division, British Army, During the Retreat from Mons.

DOING OUR 'BIT' *by Ian Hay*—Two Classic Accounts of the Men of Kitchener's 'New Army' During the Great War including *The First 100,000* & *All In It.*

AN EYE IN THE STORM *by Arthur Ruhl*—An American War Correspondent's Experiences of the First World War from the Western Front to Gallipoli-and Beyond.

STAND & FALL *by Joe Cassells*—With the Middlesex Regiment Against the Bolsheviks 1918-19.

RIFLEMAN MACGILL'S WAR *by Patrick MacGill*—A Soldier of the London Irish During the Great War in Europe including *The Amateur Army*, *The Red Horizon* & *The Great Push.*

WITH THE GUNS *by C. A. Rose & Hugh Dalton*—Two First Hand Accounts of British Gunners at War in Europe During World War 1- Three Years in France with the Guns and With the British Guns in Italy.

THE BUSH WAR DOCTOR *by Robert V. Dolbey*—The Experiences of a British Army Doctor During the East African Campaign of the First World War.

Lightning Source UK Ltd.
Milton Keynes UK
UKOW050952020512

191857UK00001B/107/P